How to ...

get th

COLES NOTES

Key Point

Basic concepts in point form.

Close Up

Additional hints, notes, tips or background information.

Watch Out!

Areas where problems frequently occur.

Quick Tip

Concise ideas to help you learn what you need to know.

Remember This!

Essential material for mastery of the topic.

Your Guide to ...

Better Golf

Driving, pitching, chipping & putting

Strategy & psychology

Tips and drills

© Copyright 1999 and Published by

COLES PUBLISHING. A division of Prospero Books

Toronto – Canada

Printed in Canada

Cataloguing in Publication Data

Kelly, Geoff, 1946 –

Your guide to ... better golf

ISBN 0-7740-0642-0

1. Golf. I. Title. II. Series

GV965.K44 1999   796.352'3   C99-9311074-7

Publisher: Nigel Berrisford
Editing: Paul Kropp Communications
Book design: Karen Petherick, Markham, Ontario
Layout: Richard Hunt
Illustration: Jin X Tang

Manufactured by Webcom Limited
Cover finish: Webcom's Exclusive DURACOAT

Contents

Introduction

There is something magical about the game of golf: it's a game that can be played in many ways, by different kinds of players with a wide range of abilities, by children, seniors and every age in between. It's a game that can be played on simple municipal greens or at world-class country clubs, with inexpensive equipment or thousand-dollar irons and drivers. But what sets a real golfer apart from the duffer or rank beginner is the urge to improve – to lower your score, take points off your handicap, to finish the 18th hole with a better score than ever before.

This book will help you reach that goal.

Beginner golfers should work with a pro, develop a style and get used to the conventions of golf. This is not a book for them.

The goal of *Better Golf* is to help middle-level golfers lower their score by five to 10 points. This requires improvement in every part of your game: better swings, better bunker play, improved greens play, optimistic mental set. Every kind of shot that presents a problem to the average golfer is discussed in detail – with tips and drills to help you improve. There are also sections on equipment, lessons, the psychology of golf and course management. Someplace in this book is a tip, reminder or concept that will help you improve your game.

Seasoned golfers know that golf is a process of constant improvement: a journey of personal and physical self discovery. If you have the opportunity to be a spectator at a PGA tournament, you will observe a phenomenon that is not apparent on television – the total focus and centering of the best players. A great golfer has the concentration of a Zen master. The intensity of that concentration is accentuated by the required silence during a shot. It is no fluke that the Japanese have embraced golf with a passion; they understand the relationship between focus, individual effort, good technique and success on the golf course.

There's a great deal of folksy wisdom about the respective value of the parts of the game such as "drive for show; putt for the dough," or "never up, never in," all based on the idea that exceptional skill at one part of the game will guarantee success. The truth is more complex. In order for an average golfer to post consistently low scores, you need to have a good solid all-round game. You need to hit the ball a decent distance off the tee without incurring penalty strokes. You need to keep the ball in the fairway towards the green with second shots and land your approach shot on the green – consistently. You need to sink the ball without three or four putting. The reason most high handicappers don't improve is because one or more parts of their game are not good.

It's usually best to concentrate on two or three areas that need improvement rather than risk your entire game. Choose the chapters you want to read based on where your game most needs work, then try the drills and fixes that are suggested. When all that has been ingrained in your "muscle memory," try to improve another aspect. By the end of a season, you'll be a much better golfer. While this book will not, by itself, get you a place on a PGA tour, it will give you the strategy and techniques to lop points off your scores.

To get started

- Keep an honest score. Otherwise you'll never know if you're really improving.
- Analyze your weaknesses and strengths. It's the weak areas that are costing you strokes.
- Choose two or three areas to work on. You can't improve your whole game at once.
- Remember that the mental game is more important than any single stroke. Stay cool and confident.

CHAPTER ONE

The swing

The swing is the basis of shot making. Before you can improve your whole game, you must develop the best swing possible. Your current swing may be generally acceptable, but you'll find something in this chapter to help improve a particular part of your swing or perhaps remind you of the fundamentals that are essential to deliver power to the ball.

Golfers are not created equal and do not develop equally, and therefore every golf swing is unique. For example, if you are a senior golfer, you may not want to focus on keeping the left heel on the ground or your left arm perfectly straight. You'll probably still hit more fairway drives than those young golfers who hit screaming drives that end up in the woods or the deep rough. The point is to use a swing that works for you. Trying to force your arm straight may create tension, and this is the last thing you need in a golf swing.

The ideal swing is just a model on which you can pattern your swing, it's not something to fastidiously copy. Have good fundamentals, but don't worry about being unique. It's your body; it's your swing.

If your swing is working for you, make only minor changes. Many golfers, some of them professionals, have ruined a good swing by trying to radically change it. If you can identify a *part* of your swing that is definitely causing a problem, or if you are regularly not hitting the fairway, then the following may be of help.

Focus Keep your mind clear of distracting thoughts. Have a swing "mantra," a thought that blocks out doubts and reinforces good swing habits. "Straight arm; follow through," "1, 2, 3 ... swing" – any phrase will do.

Just don't try to remember *everything*, the pro said, all at once.

You may have discovered a flaw in your swing and wish to focus on the correct action to fix that flaw. Then use this corrective action as your thought mantra. For instance, if you have been swinging from the outside to the inside, you might want to have the thought "inside and on the sweet spot."

PRE-SHOT ROUTINE

Golf is a game of repeated routines. This produces consistency and therefore predictable results. It is advisable to create your own pre-shot routine, a series of continuous movements that lead up to striking the ball. One pre-shot routine might go like this:

Walk up to your ball from behind on a direct path from the ball to your intended landing zone. Walk towards the ball taking the same number of steps every time, perhaps three or four. Visualize the flight of the ball, taking into consideration the wind, whether or not you will fade or draw the ball and any obstructions that may be in your path. Position your feet relative to the ball depending on which club you are using. You may wish to take a practice swing before you finally address the ball. Always take the same number of practice swings, but be aware that too many practice swings usually result in a poor shot.

Step up to the ball for the final address. Don't spend too much time at this, because it allows doubts to creep into your thoughts. Waggle the club once or twice to get yours hands and arms used to the idea that they will be in motion shortly. Look at the target. A slight forward press of the hands also sends a message that the swing is imminent and will ensure that your hands will return ahead of the ball at impact. Eye on the ball. Swing the club. Follow through.

> **Focused and concentrated on the shot.**
> **Swing easy.**

 If you get interrupted at any point in the swing process, stop and start the whole thing over, right from your pre-shot routine.

Here is a breakdown of the entire swing process. You may pick up a hint as to why you are not striking the ball as well you would like to, but when you're actually out on the golf course, your swing should be a natural event. Thinking about all the components of the swing while you're playing is a recipe for disaster. Groove your swing on the practice range so that it becomes an unconscious event on the course.

GRIP

Most golfers start with the grip that their parents or their friends or a golf pro showed them when they first picked up a club. Over time, a golfer's grip becomes second nature and is never given a second thought. But there are reasons why different grips may suit different golfers at different times. Here are the three basic grips: the overlap, interlock and baseball or ten-finger grip.

 **Overlap grip** The overlap grip is achieved by placing the left hand on the club and the pinky finger of the right hand on top of the forefinger and middle finger. This is the most common grip among amateurs and professionals. Many golfers use the overlap grip because they find the interlock and ten-finger uncomfortable.

Interlock grip Some golfers prefer the inter-lock grip because it prevents one hand from becoming dominant on the downswing. Also, people with small hands find the interlock grip more comfortable than the overlap or ten-finger grip. For the interlock grip, place your left hand on the club with the thumb on top and – as you place the right hand on the club – stick out the forefinger of your left hand and wrap the right-hand pinky finger around it, then close the grip.

Ten-finger grip Some women and senior golfers find that a ten-finger or baseball grip gives them more power. You may want to try it and see if it gives you more distance.

The most important aspect of grip is that your hands work as a unit. The second most important factor is that you don't put a "death grip" on the club. You should replace the rubber grips on your clubs every few years for precisely this reason – clubs should be held loosely so you can swing with ease. One pro describes the appropriate grip pressure as holding on to a bird just hard enough to prevent it from flying away. Another says that your grip should be like holding the steering wheel of your car. Choose a metaphor you like – the principle is always the same: no death grip. On days when your tension mounts, your grip pressure often becomes far too high.

Key thought **Grip the club lightly.**

STANCE

The stance is the basis for the golf swing. As with many sports, an athletic "ready" position is the foundation for the rest of the body to go into action. Think of a tennis player anticipating a return volley from an opponent, or a baseball outfielder waiting for a ball to be hit towards him. In both instances these athletes have their feet firmly planted, at least as wide as their shoulders, knees flexed ready to move and upper body bent forward. The same athletic stance is required in preparation for a proper golf swing. Your upper body should be flexed from the waist; your back, although bent from the waist, should be kept straight. Have a friend check out your stance at a driving range (but never on the course).

 When changing the direction of your stance, make sure you not only move your feet but your whole body – especially the hips and shoulders.

 Comfortable and solid.

SETUP

Setup refers to the positioning of the ball relative to your feet. Generally speaking, the ball is positioned towards the front of the stance for longer clubs and towards the middle or center of the stance for the shorter irons. The reason is simple: the shorter the club, the shorter the shaft, therefore the ball is progressively played closer to the golfer.

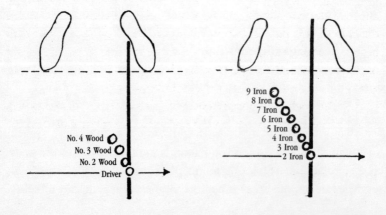

TAKEAWAY

Your takeaway should be slow with a focus on swinging the club back along the ideal return swing path. The ideal path, of course, is on a direct line with the target. A takeaway that goes outside this perfect imaginary line will return on the downswing from outside to inside, producing a slice.

It is important to keep your wrists in the same position throughout the takeaway. Any cocking of the wrist before the club reaches parallel to the ground will lead to an open club face at the top of the backswing and stay open throughout the downswing. This usually results in a slice.

 Drill Stick a tee in the ground about 16 inches behind the ball on the target line; when you take your club back make sure you knock over the tee. The path of the club head will be duplicated on your downswing, helping you to stay on plane.

 Key thought **Slow takeaway.**

Wrist cock The only way to have the club arrive at the right position behind you, and maintain a relatively straight left arm, is to have your wrists cock as the club is being taken back. This is a natural effect of the backswing and need not be done consciously. When the club shaft is parallel to the ground on the takeaway and the club head is pointing skywards, your wrists are starting to cock. As your upper body completes the turn, the wrist cock is completed. Your wrists automatically uncock on the downswing.

Wrist cock is important because it gives "snap" to the downswing and thereby speeds up the club head for greater distance.

Body turn Feet are planted firmly, shoulders and hips turn with your club on the backswing. Your left shoulder ends up directly under your chin; your right elbow rises up from your side and, at the top of the swing, points at the ground. Weight has moved to the right side of your body. At the top of the backswing the club face should be square to your right arm. Keep your knees slightly flexed, ready to transfer weight from the right to left side during the downswing.

Key thought   With feet planted, turn the body.

Weight shift Body weight, when you address the ball at the beginning of a shot, is evenly distributed on both feet. As your swing starts, there may be a slight forward press to the left, but as the club is brought back in the takeaway, your weight smoothly transfers from the left to the right side of the body. As the club is swung down, your weight transfers from the right to the left side of the body.

Smooth body turn is key to a good swing, but it is important not to let your body get ahead of the arms during the downswing movement – this leads to an open club face at impact or adjustments of the hands, which most amateurs can't do fast enough to square up the club face. Keep your arms and body in unison throughout the swing. If this seems to be a problem, best to have a pro look at your swing.

Top of the backswing The shaft should stop on the backswing when it is at a 90° angle to the extended left arm or parallel to the ground. Some pros, like John Daly, can take the club back beyond this point and achieve extra-long distance off the tee, but the average golfer rarely has the flexibility and hand-eye co-ordination to duplicate these monster drives. The main reason for this is that excessive backswing creates a destabilizing effect on the rest of your body on the downswing, which takes a great deal of co-ordination to control. So be reasonable. At the top of the backswing, your hands finish above shoulders with your thumbs under the shaft and the back of your left wrist straight, not cupped.

The goal in the backswing should be to attain a point of power and comfort. If you are having problems keeping the left arm straight, don't force it. There is nothing wrong with a slightly bent left arm. This is especially true for senior golfers who may have lost some flexibility. Other golfers find a shorter backswing is more comfortable and produces a shot that is more accurate. Practice at the driving range to find out how much backswing produces the best results for you.

 Drill Swing in front of a mirror using a shaft with no club head.

Key thought **Back faces target.**

Downswing The downswing should begin slowly. Ideally, the downswing should start with the legs and lower body, your weight beginning to move from the right to the left. Your upper body and arms uncoil using the lower body and legs as a pivot. Your right arm may rise up away from the body during the backswing, but during the downswing your right elbow should return to the right side of the body. This prevents an outside-to-inside swing path. Don't try to make adjustments on the downswing – just let it happen. The movement happens in a split second, too fast to make adjustments.

 Drill As you begin the downswing, visualize pulling down on a rope.

RELEASE

The speed of the club head picks up when your wrists uncock, beginning at about the three o'clock position. It is important, as you swing down, that your hands stay ahead of the ball at impact. (The driver is the only club where the hands are not ahead of the club head.) The amount the hands stay ahead of the ball varies with the loft of the club. As the loft of the club increases and the ball is played further back, your hands should stay in the same position regardless of how far back the ball is placed. The average high hand-icapper does not keep his hands ahead of the ball at impact; this adds loft to a club, which results in a high shot and reduced distance.

One reason the pros hit shots longer than most amateurs is that they *always* keep their hands ahead of the club head through impact. This effectively reduces the loft of the club so a pro hitting a five iron will get the normal distance of a good amateur with a four or even a three iron.

Impact If you want to gain accuracy and power for your shots, you must swing through and past the ball. Many average golfers are too eager to look up and see how straight and how far their ball is flying. This is a terrible mistake. Looking up forces your upper body to rise up, which in turn reduces the power flow. The downswing happens so fast that some golfers may not realize that they begin to look up before impact.

 Drill Without hitting balls, practice swinging through the ball and pointing the club towards the target after impact. To avoid looking up too soon, look at the back of the ball during impact.

 Key thought   **Head down. Swing through the ball.**

TEMPO

Tempo is the rhythm of the swing, how fast the whole sequence happens right from the setup. An even balance between the backswing and the downswing is important. Some pros suggest counting – "1, 2" or "1, 2, 3" (where "1" is the address position) to keep the tempo of your swing balanced and even.

Although the backswing starts slow and comes to a stop at the top of the swing, it is important not to begin with a sharp burst of speed on the downswing. A sudden burst of speed on the downswing leads to an open club head at impact – and a shot that flies off into the woods.

Rather, your swing should gradually pick up speed as it moves towards impact with the ball. The idea is to increase speed so that it reaches a maximum just when your club contacts the ball. This is what gives you maximum distance, with consistent accuracy.

Remember, rushing any part of the game of golf will be detrimental to your score. Do everything slowly before your shot; this will create a calmness that will carry over to your swing.

 Drill At the range, make a concerted effort to swing as slowly as possible, gradually increasing the speed until you are hitting the ball smoothly and solidly.

 Key thought **Slow down.**

FOLLOW-THROUGH AND FINISH

A good follow-through ensures that you are swinging through the ball. One of the best indicators that you have good follow-through is where you're facing when you finish. When you have finished your swing, your belt buckle should always be facing the target (with powerful hitters, even to the left of the target line).

Make sure your right foot is raised up off the ground with the toe providing balance, while all the weight is on the left foot. Your hands should finish above the shoulders.

 Drill When you are hitting balls at the practice range, hold your finish after every shot for a few seconds. If you are swinging under control, you should be able to maintain your balance at finish.

 Key thought **"Classic" finish.**

The previous sections break the swing into parts. Your real swing, of course, is not separate parts – it is one continuous motion that you don't have to analyze and think about. Evolve your own personal swing, keeping in mind good solid basic skills.

 Emergency repairs

On days when your swing seems to have a mind of its own, go back to the basics:

- Keep your eye on the ball.
- Slow down.
- Think "classic" finish.

CHAPTER TWO

Fix your slice

The slice is the most common problem faced by middle-level golfers. It is caused either by striking the ball with an open club face or by striking the ball with an outside-to-inside swing. The effect is the same. This type of impact induces right-hand spin to the ball, which, due to the aerodynamic nature of the dimples on a golf ball, creates a right-to-left ball flight.

Fixing the slice requires time at a driving range and some attention to fundamentals and possible problems in your swing and setup.

SWING PATH

A swing path that goes from the outside to inside (relative to the proper plane of the swing) will produce a slice. The more out-to-in you swing, the bigger your slice will be.

Here's how to check your swing path: when you are set up in your stance and addressing the ball, imagine that the ball is the face of a clock.

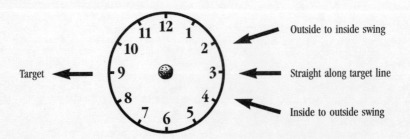

A straight shot occurs when your squared club face strikes the ball at the three o'clock position and continues through the ball towards the nine o'clock position. This stroke is squarely on a path that is parallel to the stance of the golfer and the target line. Since the exact spot at which this may occur is so small, most balls are hit either slightly to the left or right of the three o'clock position. These slightly off-center hits produce either a **fade**, a shot that curves slightly to the right of the target line, or a **draw**, which curves slightly to the left. A **slice** or **hook** occurs when the ball curves even further from the target line, a slice curving considerably to the right and a hook considerably to the left.

If your club face strikes the ball at the two o'clock position and continues through the ball towards the seven o'clock position – an outside-to-inside swing – a great deal of right-hand spin is imparted to the ball. Because of the aerodynamics created by the dimples, your ball will curve dramatically away from you in the classic "banana slice." This might be a real beauty of a shot, except for the fact that it usually ends up in the woods. In some situations, a slice will also reduce distance dramatically.

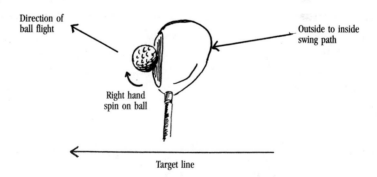

Direction of ball flight

Outside to inside swing path

Right hand spin on ball

Target line

The easiest way to check whether you are swinging on plane or not is to find a range that has one of those circular machines made out of PVC pipe against which you can check your swing. Whether on one of these machines, or with a pro or friend, check the position of the club face at the top of your backswing. The club face should be parallel to your right forearm. Another way to check the plane of your swing is to set up in front of a large mirror and have someone stick a piece of tape along the angle of the image of the club shaft on the mirror. Have this person watch for any deviations above or below this tape line while you swing the club.

Drill One way to stop swinging from the outside to the inside is to set up a piece of 2 x 6 lumber on edge about six inches away from the ball, pointing towards a target parallel to your stance. Once you are confident you are swinging properly (and in no danger of hitting the 2 x 6), set up a ball and take a full swing. With this drill, if you start swinging outside the proper swing plane, you will hit the 2 x 6 board. Ouch!

A similar drill, which doesn't require a visit to your local lumber yard, is to set up a ball and then stick two tees about six inches away from the ball at the two and seven o'clock positions. If you hit the tees, you are swinging outside to inside.

Another good way to check your swing path is to look at your divots. If they point to the left of the intended target line, you are swinging from out to in.

Key thought If you have been swinging from out to in, focus on an inside-and-through swing. Try to keep your right elbow close to the body during the downswing.

CLUB FACE OPEN

Even if you are swinging on plane, it is possible to slice the ball if your club face is open at impact. The whole idea behind curing a slice is *square*, that your swing should be right along the intended path and that your club should be perfectly perpendicular to that path at impact. If your club is open, or angled even 10° off square, you'll be sending too many balls into the woods.

Try this drill, with a bucket of balls at the driving range, to check if the angle of your club face at address is affecting the flight of the ball. Grip the club properly (refer to the section below on weak grip). Hold the club behind the ball and look at the angle of the club face. Is the line from your target square to the club face? If not, adjust it accordingly.

Try a shot and observe the flight of the ball. If the ball still slices, address the ball and close the club face a little (turn the shaft towards the target while maintaining a proper grip). Once again, strike a ball and observe the flight path. Continue to close the face of the club head and hit balls noting the flight of the balls. At some point the balls will begin to hook. This is the point to reverse the process. Begin to gradually open the club face and continue hitting balls until the hit balls fly straight ahead. Note the angle of the club face and remember it when you set up for your next shot.

Some clubs are being manufactured with a built-in closed face. If you are desperate to cure your slice by such means, you may wish to inquire about this kind of club at your local pro shop or equipment provider.

 Drill   Stand behind the ball and square the club face before addressing the ball. Hold the club head position as you set up.

 Key thought   Is my club face at address set up to produce a slice or hook, or is my club face set up to produce the kind of shot I really want?

IMPROPER GRIP

The start of your setup is the time to check your grip. Stand behind the ball looking at the intended flight path. Ground your club, place your left hand on the shaft at the top. Your thumb should be pointing down, the meaty area below your thumb (the thumb pad) on top of the club, the V between your thumb and forefinger pointing towards your right ear. There should be no gap between the thumb and forefinger. Place your right hand on the club according to the type of grip you prefer. The V created by the grip of the club by the thumb and forefinger of the right hand should also point to your right ear.

A grip with the hands pointing to the right side of the body is called a "strong" grip, to the left, a "weak" grip. A weak grip will cause an open club face at impact and your ball will fly from left to right – a slice.

To effect a cure, work on your grip at the driving range. Try adjusting your grip from strong to weak and note the effect on the ball flight. The most important thing about any grip is that it's comfortable. A strong grip is usually more natural and comfortable and will reduce the chance of slicing.

 If you are adjusting your grip, you may have to adjust only one hand rather than move both of them together. The less you have to change, the better.

Key thought Your hands must function as a unit. The grip must be tight enough to maintain control of the club, but also allow the club to be swung freely. Maintain the same grip pressure throughout the swing.

20

BALL POSITION

If the ball is placed too far forward at address, your club will contact the ball when the club head is beginning to move off the swing path. This creates an outside-to-inside path. And such a path will cause the ball to slice.

 Drill Place a club on the ground parallel to the desired ball flight. Place another club at right angles to this club. Tee up a ball in line with the second club. Set up your stance so that your heel touches the club pointing at your ball. Strike the ball and observe the flight path. Set up the ball a little further back in your stance (maintain your heel next to the club on the ground) and strike the ball observing the effect of each change in ball position.

Key thought Make sure you are looking at the *back* of the ball when the club head strikes it.

SETUP

An open stance, one that is set up to the left of the target, will produce an out-to-in swing. As we have seen, this gives you a slice.

Drill Check the alignment of your stance with the target by placing a club across your chest and then turn your head to see where the club is pointing.

Release Once your arms and hands reach the nine o'clock position (about waist high) on the downswing, they rotate so that the right hand eventually goes over the left hand as you swing through the impact. Check your hands after you have struck the ball – if your right hand is under the left, the club face will be open and the resulting shot will slice.

Most golfers who slice release their wrists too early in the downswing. If your club is gripped too tightly, the arms and wrists may be too stiff to release properly. A good drill to check that your club head is closing through impact is to take practice swings with your driver at half speed and focus on the gradual turning of your right arm over the left arm. The *back* of your right hand should always be facing the sky at finish.

 Key thought **The club face opens through the backswing, begins closing on the downswing and closes on the follow-through. Right hand is over left at finish.**

HOOKS

Hooks are shots that curve considerably to the left of the intended line of flight. The causes are the opposite of those for a slice. An inside-to-outside swing plane will impart left-hand spin on the ball and therefore a right-to-left flight. A closed club face at impact will also impart left-hand spin on a ball and right-to-left flight.

Hooking is a problem usually experienced by advanced golfers because they are doing some aspect of a cure for the slice to excess. If you end up hooking the ball, review the above with especial attention to any late release and excessive body turn on the follow-through. Swinging excessively inside the swing plane can cause a hook. A closed club face at address will result in a closed club face at impact, causing a hook.

Hooking is generally a lot easier to remedy than a slice. As a matter of fact, there are many slicers who give *anything* to know what it feels like to hook the ball.

PULLS AND PUSHES

Pulls are shots that fly straight to the left of the intended line of flight. They are caused by the ball set up too far forward in the stance.

Pushes fly straight, but to the right. Pushes mean that you are swinging from the inside of the plane to the outside, so adjust your swing accordingly. You may also try moving the ball forward in the stance so that the ball is struck as the club head moves towards the finish.

A last resort If all else fails, buy a club with a built-in closed face. One such club is designed with a 2˚ open face to help those who hook the ball, the second club is a square face and the third has a 2˚ closed face. Your pro shop will have sample clubs that you can try out before purchasing.

 Many golfers fade the ball; those who fade the ball excessively are slicers. A controlled fade is a desirable shot, and those slicers who have learned to reduce their slices and have confidence in their fade can use it effectively on the golf course. If you have a consistent fade, set up on the right side of the tee box - you'll have more fairway to play with

CHAPTER THREE

Fairway shots

Every part of the game of golf has its own special techniques. Perfecting your swing will certainly help both your drive and your fairway shots, but there are certain problems that pertain only to fairway play. Since this is likely to be 20 percent of your game, it's worth mastering these special situations.

SIDE-HILL LIE
Feet below the ball Even though you may hit a ball relatively long and straight from the tee, you may end up on the side of a hill. You can still execute a good shot, but you'll have to adjust your usual one.

When playing from a side-hill lie, there are three key areas that you need to concentrate on: alignment, setup and balance.

Correct **alignment** is crucial to execute this shot well. Your ball will hook so **aim to the right** of your target. The tendency to hook will increase when more power is applied to the ball; therefore don't strike the ball with all your force. You will be standing farther away from the ball in this situation; therefore your swing must be on a flatter plane to reach the ball. You'll be swinging your club around your body, rather than up and down.

A wide stance is necessary to maintain your balance. **Set up** so that the ball is positioned in the middle of your stance. There will be a tendency to fall back onto your right foot, which may produce a hook or a topped shot, so start with your weight on the left foot at the setup. Take a few practice swings and adjust your alignment and stance. When you take your shot, you want to have the confidence that you will finish in a **balanced** position. Since you will be stretching to reach the ball, hold the club at the very end of the grip.

Feet above the ball Since you are standing uphill from the ball, there is a tendency to fall off balance - forward - during the swing. Counteract this by keeping your weight on your heels. You will be standing closer to the ball than usual and therefore your swing will be more upright. The ball will have a tendency to fly to the right, not a slice, but a push. Counteract this by **aiming to the left** of your target.

> **Key thought** **Key thoughts for hill lies – swing easy and keep your balance.**

THE FIRST CUT OF ROUGH

If your ball is sitting up on top of the grass, play it as a normal shot. This can actually be a great advantage if you have a long shot to the green. Play the ball forward in your stance and hit it as if the ball were sitting on a tee. Sweep it off the grass.

If your ball is buried in the grass, "in the cabbage," do not attempt to strike the ball with a long iron. Long irons have a sharp leading edge that does not slide easily through the grass. **Fairway woods** are rounded and smooth on the bottom and therefore slide easily through grass. This situation is the perfect time to use a lofted wood such as a five or seven wood. Play the ball slightly back in the stance, then hit down on the ball. The loft will drive the ball up and provide height to your shot; the smooth sole of the club will slide through the grass.

 Aim to hit about an inch behind the ball.

> **Key thought** **Select the right club and set up to the ball according to the lie.**

FAIRWAY BUNKERS

The main challenge of hitting out of a fairway bunker is getting a solid footing. Shuffle your feet back and forth with your weight towards the insteps of your feet. Since you won't have the kind of stability you experience on the fairway, you won't be able to maintain your balance with a full swing. The solution is to swing as you would normally, with a full body turn, but shorten both your backswing and follow-through. Since you have buried your feet in the sand, shorten up your grip on the club an equal amount.

It is important to get as much distance as possible in your hit from a fairway bunker; therefore focus on picking the ball cleanly from the sand. The more sand you take, the less distance you will achieve.

Play the ball a little back from your normal stance for the club you are using. This will improve your chances of hitting the ball, not the sand. If you have a good lie you can take a four iron and pick the ball cleanly off the sand, or if the shot requires more loft use a fairway wood.

 Make sure you select a club that will provide enough height to clear the far lip of the bunker.

PLAYING INTO THE WIND

A head or cross wind will have a negative effect on the distance and direction of a shot. The knock-down or punch shot will help solve this dilemma.

The object with this shot is to maintain a low trajectory and to have the ball roll once it lands.

Move the ball back in your stance, slightly to the right of center. As a result, the ball is struck earlier in the swing and your club is, in effect, delofted. Stand a little closer to the ball; this helps maintain a square club face at impact (otherwise you may hook this shot). Choke down on the grip slightly; this reduces the flex of the club, which helps keep the ball low. Shorten your backswing so backspin is reduced, which makes the ball fly higher.

As in all shots make sure your hands are ahead of the ball. As the backswing was shortened, so should the follow-through. This helps maintain a smooth rhythm. Your practice swing should include all of the above changes to your normal full swing so you'll be ready to take the appropriate shot.

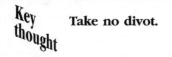

Key thought   **Shorter backswing and shorter follow-through.**

WET FAIRWAY

Another place to use the knock-down or punch shot is on a wet fairway. Wet fairways present special problems for golfers. First, there is no bounce if a club strikes the ground behind the ball. Second, any moisture picked up by the club before contact with the ball will interfere with proper ball flight. It is therefore important to ensure solid contact with the ball.

The punch shot technique is similar to that above. Play the ball back in your stance a little more than usual. Shorten your swing, use more club than normal, pick the ball as cleanly as possible from the grass. Your ball will fly lower with more spin.

Key thought   **Take no divot.**

Blind shots When the landing area of your shot is blocked, it is important to stop and figure out how you are going to get the ball where you want it rather than just blasting away in the general direction. Don't be reluctant to walk up and figure out the line. Pick an intermediate spot on the line and aim for it.

Approach shots Many high handicappers miss greens by underclubbing on the approach shot or not hitting the ball hard enough to reach the green. If you notice that you are constantly coming up short of the green, take an extra club and hit it full. You will have confidence that the target will be reached and therefore won't be tempted to kill the ball.

Getting out of trouble When you get into trouble, it is important not to compound the negative effect on your score. Consider the reward factor for trying a difficult low-percentage shot, and also the penalty if you flub it or end up in more trouble.

If you are playing well and a difficult shot may give you a chance at a birdie, go for it. But if your round is not going well, forget about trying a hard shot and choose a shot that will only cost one stroke, such as a pitch out to the fairway. Nothing depresses a golfer more than being in trouble and either staying in the same trouble due to a flubbed shot, or hitting into more trouble.

IN THE WOODS

When your ball lands in the trees, it is important to think the situation through so you won't make a mistake that will add strokes to your score. If there is no line towards the hole or the lie prevents a swing, take a stroke for an unplayable lie. You may drop the ball within two club lengths of the line between the ball and the hole. While you can position no closer to the hole, you can go as far back along the line of the ball and the hole as you want. A good drop can keep you from losing yet another stroke.

If you have a playable lie in the woods, you may either choose to pitch out sideways to the fairway or try to advance your ball through an opening towards the green. If the route out to the fairway is a certain shot, this is usually the simplest and smartest choice. If you choose to hit the ball through a narrow opening to the green, consider the risk/reward of such a difficult shot. The expression "trees are 90 percent air" is only true when you don't have to hit through one.

If you are off-line and hit a tree, you may end up in a worse situation. Use a punch shot, as described previously, so the ball will come out low and tend to bounce and roll a lot after landing. If there are water and sand hazards around the green, don't even try for the green. Even without hazards, a low rolling shot is almost impossible to stop on the green. You may want to try for a landing in front of the green on the fairway.

Since a shot from the woods usually has to fly from beneath branches, hit a low-flying shot:

- Use the longest iron you have (some players carry a one iron solely for this shot).
- Choke up on the grip.
- Open your stance.
- Play the ball off your right foot.
- Shorten both your swing and follow-through.

Hitting off pine needles or leaves You may legally improve your chances in the woods by removing twigs and sticks. Should you move the ball during this process you will be penalized, so be careful.

If you have the line of flight for a high shot, consider using a sand shot from pine needles or leaves. Use an upright swing and hit about an inch behind the ball. This is a tough shot, so get familiar with it during practice.

DISTANCE TO THE HOLE

Once you know how far you can hit with each club consistently, it becomes important to know how far you need to hit the ball. Is it 150 or 160 yards to the hole? Most courses provide some aid to making distance estimates. Almost every course will have a blue 200 yard marker, a white 150 yard marker and a red 100 yard marker. Some courses also plant a particular species of tree at the 200 and 150 yards points on the course. The starter will (should) advise you of any distance aids.

As well, sprinkler heads are often marked with yardage to the center of the green. Take the time to use this information if it's available. Walk to the sprinkler head or marker, pace off back to your ball, then make the calculation.

Remember to take into consideration the placement of the hole. If the flag is positioned on the **middle** of the stick, the hole is in the center of the green; when it's at the **bottom** of the flag stick, it's at the front of the green; and if the flag is at the **top** of the stick, the hole is at the back of the green. These green distances may vary by as much as 20 or 30 yards.

If you are consistently miscalculating distances, you may wish to buy an optical laser range-finding device, basically a pair of binoculars with a laser sight. They are expensive, but you'll know for sure how far it is to the hole and also how far you have hit any particular shot. Some courses also have devices installed on golf carts that display the distance to the hole plus many kinds of other useful information.

CHAPTER FOUR

The short game

For any golfer, 70 percent of your shots will be from a position closer than 100 yards to the flag. The bad news, as you know, is that this is where most golfers run up their scores. The good news is that a little work on the short game will enable you to improve your game considerably.

PITCHING AND CHIPPING

The main difference between pitching and chipping is the trajectory of the ball. Most golfers think of the **pitch** as a short high shot that stops quickly after it lands and a **chip** as a short low shot that rolls after it lands. Pitching is generally harder to do than chipping, so chip whenever possible.

While pitching is ordinarily done with a nine iron, pitching wedge or sand wedge, almost any iron can be used to chip. Clubs with some loft - from the seven iron to wedge - are more commonly used because the loft helps to get the ball up. However, even a three wood can be used to chip, as you will see below.

If you are an inconsistent chipper, try using one club for all chipping, such as a seven or eight iron. Once you can depend on a single club for a variety of distances and conditions, you may become a one club wonder around the greens.

The conditions under which you will be pitching and chipping vary depending on where the ball lands. Specific chipping and pitching techniques will therefore vary according to the circumstance.

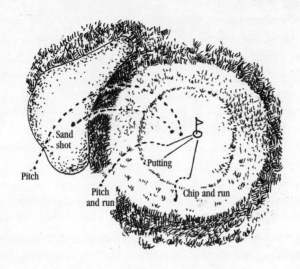

Sand
shot

Pitch

Putting

Pitch
and run

Chip and run

CHIPPING TECHNIQUE

Chipping out of long grass around the green Play the ball off your back foot with a narrow stance. Ground the club behind the ball, then close the club a little and lift the heel of the club head off the ground slightly. This setup will produce a slightly right-to-left flight; therefore aim to the right of the intended landing spot. With wrists firm, swing down sharply and strike the back of the ball. Follow through according to the amount of your backswing.

Chipping off the fringe around the green If you are just a few feet off the green, on short rough or the fringe; use a narrow but open stance. Your wrists should be firm with the arms locked in a triangle; as a result, the swing motion comes from the shoulders.

This shot is like a putt except that the loft of the club will pop your ball up. Once again, more backswing will produce more distance. Therefore it is important to practice this stroke so that the proper amount of backswing is used.

Do not decelerate on the forward stoke. Sweep the ball off the grass and finish low, about as long as the backswing.

Chipping with a three wood or sand wedge As crazy as it sounds, there are some very good reasons to consider chipping with a three wood. The three wood works in this case for the same reasons it is a good choice in the rough off the fairway. The loft of the club will get your ball up enough to skim over the grass and the smooth sole of the club will slide over the grass.

Here's how to do it. Choke up on the club, take a narrow stance and play the ball off the right foot. Then strike down on the ball with a wristy shot. Make sure you provide enough power so that once the ball clears the grass it will roll to the hole.

Use this shot if you are 12 inches or less from the edge of the green in the first cut of rough, but try it first at the practice green.

Blading Another shot that can be useful from thick grass around the green is to strike the ball with the front edge of your sand wedge. This is called "blading" the ball. You may have done this by accident out of a trap with unwelcome results. Use the same setup as you would with a normal chip; focus on the leading edge of the club striking the ball at the equator. Make sure the club is raised up so that it does not go under the ball.

Chipping off the fairway You may play this shot several ways. If you are close enough to the green, the fairway is short and smooth and the shot is not uphill, you may elect to **putt** the ball. (See the section below on the Texas wedge for a more detailed discussion of this shot.) Make sure you calculate for the effect of the fringe and fairway on the speed of the ball. The other option is to execute a short chip.

The easiest chipping club for most golfers is a seven or eight iron. The important thing to consider is where you want the ball to land so that it will release and roll towards the hole. The swing for this type of shot must be practiced so that you will know how far the ball will fly with different amounts of backswing.

Think of the club shaft as the hand of a clock: address it at six o'clock. As you swing back, the club shaft passes seven o'clock, eight o'clock and so on. Once you have practiced chipping with different amounts of backswing, learning how far the ball will fly and roll, you need only apply that knowledge for the different distances your ball lies from the hole. The setup and swing are the same as from the short rough.

Bump and run If you are chipping directly onto the green and the ball is ending up way past the hole, you need to rethink your strategy. To reach the hole, some chips require that the ball land off the green and roll onto it; this is called a bump-and-run shot.

 As a general rule, your ball will roll two-thirds as far as it flies through the air, depending on the loft of the club you are using.

Chipping into the wind The knock-down shot is useful when hitting into the wind, or for when you have too much club and you wish to control distance. This shot must be learned; therefore get it down pat at the range before trying it during play.

The knock-down shot requires a different swing than that of a regular golf shot. The trick to keeping your shot low is to inhibit your leg movement. To do so, take a stance with your feet about shoulder-width apart. Place the ball back in your stance for a low-ball trajectory, keep your weight on your left side, aim slightly left, swing with the wrists quiet and with equal backswing and follow-through. Keep your hands ahead of the ball for less loft.

 Drill Stick a tee in the ground and place a ball about an inch behind it. Take a couple of practice swings so that the low point of the arc of your swing is at the tee. Set up to hit the tee, then swing through and strike the ball as your club continues on to hit the tee. Remember to keep your hands ahead of the ball.

THE BASIC PITCH

Although the pitch from the fairway to the green should be the reward for a good drive and a good fairway shot, it is common for this shot to come up short or fly off to either side of the green. Either mistake will add extra strokes to your score.

Pitching is characterized by a high shot that lands on the green and rolls a short distance. For this reason a more lofted club – from the nine iron through the wedges – is used for pitching. When pitching, don't choke up on the grip as you do in chipping – use the full length of club. To adjust for distance, adjust the length of your backswing.

The only way to find out how far you are going to hit the ball with different amounts of backswing is to go out to the range and hit balls. Use the "clock" practice described previously to figure your own distances.

In taking a practice swing for a pitch, most golfers will just clip the grass to avoid taking a divot. This is the shot you need to make when you are striking the ball itself. Remember, focus on striking the ball first – any divot happens after the ball has been struck.

Chili dipping Too steep of a swing angle will cause your club to dig into the ground before it hits the ball, resulting in a "chunked" shot and poor distance. This is called "chili dipping," since the scooping effect is much like digging into a bowl of chili. A smart golfer reserves this technique for the restaurant.

Scooping Some players try to assist the upward arc of the ball by scooping under the ball. This results in the ball popping up – and not flying the full distance. Many pitches fall short of the green for this reason. Scooping is caused by hitting the ball below the equator. For a proper pitch, strike the ball at or above the equator with a descending blow.

A good way to understand the flight of a pitch is to take a ball in your right hand and throw it underhand so that the ball lands on the green. Experiment throwing the ball different distances and note how far it will roll. When you practice hitting shots with a club, try to imitate the ball's flight when you were throwing it.

 For greater accuracy keep your right wrist bent and your left wrist slightly curved through impact. Do not rotate your arms as you would in a full swing

Distance is not controlled by how hard you swing at the ball, it is controlled by varying the amount of backswing and follow-through. Once again, this is where you must experiment at the range. A bad lie requires more club. If you are in a bad lie, use one club more than you normally would.

The only time you should use a lob shot is when you have a perfect lie. You may wish to play this shot like a sand shot, with the club face and stance open. This produces a high lob; the only problem is that this type of shot sometimes does not carry far enough. Opening up a lob wedge and taking a full swing makes for a difficult shot.

TEXAS WEDGE

Whenever possible use your putter from well off the green; it offers a higher chance of success for most golfers than either a chip or pitch. In Texas, short closely mowed fringes around the greens are common, and when the putter is used off the green (rather than the more conventional sand wedge or short iron), it is called the Texas wedge.

As with any shot, take your time around the green and consider all the factors that will affect your shot. Check out the slope and break and other conditions on the green (see the next chapter). Select a target on the green where you want the ball to begin to roll. Raise the putter off the ground an inch to prevent snagging the grass. Stroke the putt smoothly, as you would with your normal putter stroke. Hit down on the ball to make the ball pop up and bounce a few feet. As you would with your short irons, place your hands slightly ahead of the ball at address, since this will help the downward blow.

Practice this shot before using it during actual play; you may find it useful at least once or twice during the average round.

CHAPTER FIVE

Sand shots

Most amateur golfers groan when their approach shot lands in a sand bunker. Professional players, on the other hand, sometimes intentionally land in a bunker to avoid other more difficult landing spots. They are confident that they can play out of the sand for an up and down, or possibly sink their ball right from the trap. How is it that a shot that gives most amateurs a major anxiety attack is so welcome to a pro? The pros know it's the easiest shot in the game. The sand shot is the only shot where you don't have to make direct contact with the ball.

For observers, the sand trap is one place where many variations in technique may be seen. Some players attempt to chip, pitch or putt balls out of sand traps, with varying stances and varying degrees of success. The inability of some players to hit a proper shot from a green side bunker is usually the effect of incorrect technique or using an improper club. Both problems are relatively easy to fix.

THE SAND WEDGE

In order to play the sand shot properly, you must have a sand wedge. The sand wedge was invented in the 1930s by Gene Sarazen. He wanted to create a club that would drive the ball up as he drove the club down. To achieve this, Sarazen took his niblick, the most lofted club in the 1930s (approximately a nine iron), and soldered a curved lead flange to the bottom of it. The flange allowed his club to bounce through sand or grass, rather than digging in.

Sarazen's original sand iron had a 56° loft and a 64° lie with 10° bounce. It measured 35½ inches long and had a swing weight of D6. This club has been reproduced in many variations ever since, but the principle has remained the same.

Playing sand traps When you walk into the trap and prepare to address the ball, wiggle your feet into the sand. This gives you a firm footing, lowers your body to the level of the ball, and will also tell you how much sand there is in the spot where the ball is lying. Wiggling your feet will also tell you how compact the sand is – some traps get as hard as rock after a rainfall and a drying out.

If you encounter a bunker in which the sand is hard or thin, do not use a wedge with a great deal of "bounce." Sand wedges and lob wedges have the greatest bounce to keep them from digging into the sand (see chapter 8 for more on this), but a wedge with too much bounce may rebound off a hard sand surface. As a result, the leading edge of the club will strike the ball near the equator and you'll get a thin shot that flies way over the green.

One thing that makes hitting out of a sand trap a challenge is that not all shots from sand traps are equal. Sand traps are bowl-like depressions in the ground, and therefore a ball landing in a sand trap will land with many different lies. A ball in a sand trap may have a **level and flat** lie if it lands or rolls to the center of the trap, a **downhill** lie, an **uphill** lie, or be at the very **top of the trap** either at the back or front of the hazard.

Balls may also be sitting up on top of the sand or plugged in the dreaded "fried egg" lie. Here are ways to deal with these sand shots.

BASIC SAND SHOT

Use this when your ball is in the **center** of the sand trap, sitting up **on top** of the sand on **level** ground.

There are 10 steps to the basic sand shot:

1. Address the ball in the middle of your stance. Wiggle your feet for footing.

2. Flex your knees.
3. Choke up your grip on the club, open up the face of the club and open up your stance.
4. Look at the place on the green where you want the ball to land and line up accordingly.
5. Focus your eyes on the sand **behind** the ball; do not look at the ball!
6. Your swing should be U-shaped so your club will strike the sand behind the ball and slice under the ball.
7. Take a full backswing and on the downswing strike the sand where you are looking (behind the ball).
8. Do not decelerate as you swing down on the ball.
9. Follow through.
10. As you follow through, keep looking down at the spot where your club has struck the sand.

If you are still having trouble making the basic sand shot, try this: after you have finished your shot, look at the club head. If you can look directly at the club face, you have kept the club face open; if not, concentrate on keeping the club face open throughout the swing.

 A ball struck from a wet sand trap flies considerably further than a ball struck from dry sand.

The farther away you are from the hole, the farther you will want the ball to fly; therefore you must take less and less sand as the distance to the hole increases. Hit balls at the practice sand trap, taking different amounts of sand, to get a sense of what works for you and your clubs.

The secret to becoming a good sand player is practice. Throw a bucket of balls in the practice trap and start hitting them out. Step on a few to mimic a buried ball. After all the practice balls have been hit out of the trap, chip them back in and start all over again. Before long you won't have to worry about landing in a sand trap because you'll know how to get out every time.

The four principles of successful sand play

1. Open your stance.
2. Club face is open.
3. Swing hard and follow through.
4. Take plenty of sand.

FRIED-EGG LIE

Use this when your ball is in the **center** of the sand trap, buried with only the top showing (fried egg).

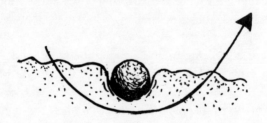

You can try this shot with your sand wedge, but if the ball is deeply imbedded use a nine iron. With either club do not open the face, still take plenty of sand, swing hard and complete your backswing.

UPHILL LIE

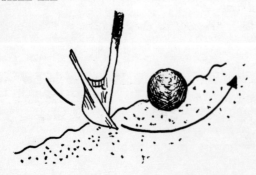

Adjust your body so that your shoulders are on an angle that matches the slope of the sand. This often requires bending the left knee (or right knee for lefties). Your weight naturally loads to the downhill side of your body. Play the ball forward in your stance, then strike the sand **closer** to the ball. Finish your follow-through high with the club pointing straight up.

DOWNHILL LIE

In a downhill lie, your weight is loaded to the left leg (right for lefties). Though the angles will look bad – and suggest you might be better off taking the penalty strokes – don't give up. You can hit out of the bunker, but don't worry about the trajectory of the ball. If you execute the swing properly, the ball will clear the top of the opposite side of the trap.

The trick – strike the sand **further behind** the ball, at least two inches.

 On either uphill or downhill lies in a sand bunker, you must position your body with the slope so that your swing will be with the slope, just as if you were on level ground.

EXPLOSION PUNCH SHOT

If your ball is at the very top of the trap, just beneath the lip, you may need to strike the ball with an explosion punch shot. This is not as difficult as it sounds. Address and swing are the same as above, but you will not be able to follow through. The hard swing, impact of the club on the sand and the short distance your club travels under the ball will explode the ball up and out of the trap. Unfortunately, the ball may not carry as far as you would like.

If you feel this shot is impossible, you may want to chip the ball backwards into the trap, where you can execute a normal sand shot.

LOB WEDGE

The L-wedge is a club that can make coming out of the sand even easier than a sand wedge. L-wedges have more loft, a bigger flange and more bounce than a standard sand wedge. When used as described above, they are virtual "no brainers" out of the sand. Just follow the four principles of sand play.

PUTTING OUT OF A HIGH BUNKER

Occasionally you may encounter a sand trap that is higher than the green, with a low lip, where the sand is fairly firm and the grass between the trap and the green is short and smooth. In this situation, you may want to putt out of the trap. You must, of course, strike the ball firmly enough to clear the trap lip and carry through any grass to the green and then have the ball roll towards the hole. This is another great shot to practice before you try it on the course.

Check the green first

Before hitting out of a sand trap, walk up to the green and figure out where you want the ball to land on the green. If the pin is located so that you have a small amount of green to play, you may wish to direct your shot to a larger part of the green. Although you may be a little farther from the pin, you will have more chance of staying on the green.

CHAPTER SIX

Putting

Putting has been called a game within a game. With the smooth, velvet surface of modern greens and the finesse of many golfers in putting shots, the action on the green might seem more closely related to billiards than golf. This concept did not escape a player in the early years of golf who used a pool cue to putt his shots on the green, a practice that was quickly outlawed by the authorities.

Since more shots are putted in a round of golf than any other type of shot, it is important to become a good, consistent putter to score well. A good putter will one- and two-putt, high handicappers end up two-, three- and four-putting their score into the stratosphere.

A good putter who is mediocre off the tee and on the fairway will still beat a long-ball hitter who is lousy on the greens – every time.

Good putting is a combination of "feel" and sound fundamentals. Feel is a natural ability to judge the direction and speed of a putt. All of us have a certain amount of feel and this ability is enhanced with practice and playing experience. Feel is often not enough to ensure consistent success. When feel fails, it is important to have a good grasp of putting fundamentals. The following sections will discuss how to check the line of your putt and factors that will affect the roll of the ball.

CHECKING THE LINE OF A PUTT

If you are not "away" on the green, spend some time figuring out how your ball is going to react to the contours of the green. Putts may be uphill, downhill; break left, break right; or any combination of these. After your approach shot, as you are walking up to the green, start to figure out the lay of the land. Remember, you can see the slopes of a green better off the green than when you are on it.

Decide on a line and stick with it. Walk up the line towards the hole and check for any anomalies such as ball marks, spike marks or debris. You can fix ball marks and remove debris such as leaves, but according to the rules you can't fix spike marks, so figure them into your calculations. Walk around the hole and survey the line from the other side of the hole. This should reinforce your first impression. Getting right down on your hands and knees to look at the line gives you a more realistic view of the terrain from the ball to the hole.

Greens will generally slope away from higher elevations and towards large ponds or lakes.

Once you have decided on the line of a putt, plumb bobbing is a good way to check which way a putt will break. Before playing, find out where you have to hold your putter so that it will hang vertically. (Due to the various designs of putter heads, the shaft will not automatically hang straight down.) Experimenting at home by sighting the shaft along a perpendicular line such as a door jam, you will find out where to hold the putter so that it hangs straight down. On the green, stand behind the ball in a line towards the hole, then hold your putter up and focus on the ball with your dominant eye. Glance up from the ball to the hole. The difference between the hole and the club shaft indicates the amount and direction of the break.

PUTTING FUNDAMENTALS

Stance The putting stroke differs from other golf shots in that your lower body is kept still and the force of a putt comes from the shoulders and arms.

To set up, your feet should be relatively close together. Stand close to the ball so that you can look down at the ball and your eyes are directly over the line of the putt. (You can check this by taking a ball while you are set up to putt, holding it at your eyes and dropping it.) In the setup position, you should be able to glance sideways down the line of the putt and back to your ball to make final adjustments in aim. Your feet are either directly ahead at right angles to the line of the putt or your leading foot may be slightly open (especially on long putts).

If you are still having problems aiming your putts, there are a variety of aiming aids you may purchase at the pro shop. Laser aiming devices are the quickest way to tell where your club face is pointing. Of course, these are illegal during tournament play, but they can be quite useful when you're practicing.

Grip There is much individual variation in putting grips. Some players use the same grip that they use for all golf shots, but this approach is not recommended. The putting stroke is different from your regular stroke so muscle memory from your regular stroke can interfere with your putting stroke. For this reason, some golfers change to a **cross-handed grip** when putting, with the left hand below the right. This reinforces the pendulum motion and prevents your right hand from taking over at the moment of impact.

Another variation on the regular grip is the **reverse overlap grip**. Rather than have the index finger overlapping the knuckles of the left hand, the index finger of the right hand overlaps the knuckles of the left hand. Both thumbs should be placed on top of the shaft.

Regardless of the grip, most golfers choke down on the putter to obtain maximum accuracy in the stroke.

Stroke One of the main differences between putting and other golf shots is that a putted ball rolls along the ground rather than goes flying through the air. Moreover, a good putt **rolls** towards the hole – it does not bounce or skitter. The best roll is end-over-end, which ensures that the putt stays on the chosen line. End-over-end roll is achieved when the ball is struck smoothly, slightly above the equator of the ball.

Your putting stroke should be at least the same distance back as forward. If there is any difference in the forward and backward movement of the putter head, it should be towards a more forward stroke. Many weak golfers take the putter head back too far; on the downstroke they realize that they are going to hit the ball too hard and decelerate the putter head. Deceleration results in little or no follow-through, thereby reducing the roll of the ball. A ball that does not roll will often not make it to the hole and has a tendency to veer off its line. A firmly hit putt with good roll will get to the hole and stay on course.

Take a couple of practice swings until you feel that you have the right amount of backswing and follow-through to provide the power to reach the hole. Your practice strokes also need to duplicate the squareness of the putter head to the line of the putt.

If you want the ball to travel farther, swing the putter back more. Do not apply more power to the stoke to attain more distance.

 Key thought **Lower body stays still; pendulum swing with the arms.**

If you look up to see where your putt is going, you will usually push to the right of the hole. Concentrate on looking at the impact spot on the ball – and *keep looking* at that spot after the ball has been struck.

 Drill If you find yourself looking up as soon as you strike the ball, spend some time putting without a target on the practice green.

You will often see pros marking their ball, cleaning it and resetting it so that the logo or manufacturer's name is positioned to become the target for impact.
Try it yourself.

Long breaking putts Putts with large breaks, either to the right or the left, are some of the most difficult shots to make. It is difficult to convince yourself that you need to aim at a target that is four or more feet above the hole in order for it to arrive at the hole. A useful question to ask in this situation is, if I hit my ball directly at the hole, where will it likely end up? Make the necessary calculation before setting up over your ball and stick with it throughout the shot. Your gut feeling is never as smart as what your head has carefully figured out.

Drill On the practice green, find a hole with a large break. Figure out a line you want to putt and an intermediate target. Walk over to the intermediate target and stick a tee in the spot, go back and make the putt, and observe the result. If the putt is successful (either in the hole or within inches), try some more putts along the same line. If the putt is unsuccessful, pick another intermediate target and mark it with a tee, and try again.

Short putts Nothing is more disheartening than missing a short putt. Many players miss short putts because they don't take enough time to line up short putts as carefully as long putts. Carelessness always costs.

Use the same stance, grip and stroke as with long putts. Unless you're playing for a trophy or money, forget about "gimmes." Taking gimmes gets you out of practice for making short putts when you need them.

Many short putts are missed to the left of the hole because most amateurs swing from an open putter face on the backswing to a closed putter face on the follow-through. It's important to concentrate on keeping the face of your putter square to the line of the putt.

If there is a break to a short putt, it can be hard to ignore the hole when lining up. Pick a target close to the hole and aim the ball at it, try to blank out the hole from your mind and focus on the target.

It is important to stroke short putts with authority so that the ball has a chance of dropping in the hole and also so that spike marks and any slopes around the hole do not take control of the ball.

 Drill On the practice green, find a hole with a break. Circle the hole about two feet out with six balls evenly spaced. Putt the balls in sequence. Keep trying until you get them all in one after the other.

Lag putts When your shot to the green lands 30 or 40 feet away from the hole, it is important that if you don't sink the putt, the next shot is at least within four feet of the cup. This way you have a good chance of two-putting rather than leaving a six to eight footer (or more) that has less chance of going in.

Golfing activity on the greens focuses on the hole; as a result, the grass at the hole has had more trampling and is thinner than the grass 30 or 40 feet away. You must take this into consideration when deciding how hard you will hit a long putt – otherwise your putt may go past the hole a considerable distance.

Key thought **Reach the general area of the hole (don't fantasize about sinking the ball).**

Drill Set up with four balls 30 or 40 feet away from the hole. Think of the hole as a barrel, about three feet wide. Set up over your ball and aim towards the hole. See how many putts you can get within 18 inches of the hole.

Going to school Going to school means learning from someone else's putt. If another player's ball is outside your ball on the green, he is required to putt first. If his ball is on a similar line to yours, it is important to watch how his ball rolls. This will help you understand the roll and slope of the green. Even if the other player's putt is on an entirely different line from yours, you will still learn something about the general slope of the green by observing how the ball rolls towards the hole. Keep in mind that you cannot stand directly behind the putter or on the line past the cup to watch. But once the ball has been struck, it is perfectly okay to walk up to the line and watch how the ball moves.

Optical illusions Beware of greens on hilly courses or next to steep cliffs. These situations can create optical illusions where what looks like a downhill putt is uphill, or a left-hand break is really a right-hand break. Lookout Golf Club near St. Catharines, Ontario, offers a good example of this phenomenon. Local knowledge is priceless in dealing with tricky optical situations; don't be embarrassed to ask a member of a hilly course about the break of a putt.

Uphill putts and downhill putts

It's a lot easier to make an uphill putt than a downhill putt. Try to land your approach shot below the flag stick and leave lag putts with an uphill putt remaining to the hole. On an uphill putt, grip the putter firmly and stroke confidently. On a downhill putt grip the putter lightly, stroke slowly and pray.

CONDITION OF GREENS

The most useful part of your pre-game routine may be time spent on the practice green before teeing off. Even if you don't have time to warm up at the driving range, try to get in a few putts before you tee off. Although practice greens are not an exact copy of the greens on the course, you will get an idea of the type and length of grass you will be playing on. You may also get a sense of the moisture level of the grass and soil.

Wet greens are slower than **dry** greens, and dry greens are harder than wet greens. During any particular round of golf you are certain to encounter greens that are either wet or dry. Greens during the early hours of the day will tend to be wetter than later in the day when the sun has had a chance to dry them out. Greens at lower elevations will tend to be wetter than greens at higher elevations. Once you have settled in your own mind whether a green is wet or dry, you will be able to adjust the power of your putts accordingly.

GRAIN

The grain of the grass on greens refers to the overall direction of grass growth. Balls will roll slower against the grain and have a tendency to move off the line of the putt. Conversely, balls roll faster with the grain and stay on the line more easily.

The easiest place to check the grain is at the hole around the rim of the cup. If the grass seems to fall off into one side of the hole more than another, it's probably growing from that direction. Another indication of the grain of the putting surface is how light reflects from it. If a putting surface appears shiny, the grain is growing away from where you are standing. A ball will roll more easily on this surface than from the opposite side. If the surface appears dull, the grain is likely growing towards you and a putt will meet some resistance from the grain. The grain can increase the effect of a break or decrease it, depending on which way it grows relative to the break.

If you are putting with the grain, and you miss and go past the hole, you have to remember that you are putting against the grain to come back.

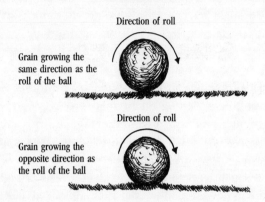

Direction of roll

Grain growing the same direction as the roll of the ball

Direction of roll

Grain growing the opposite direction as the roll of the ball

Most golfers don't spend as much time practicing putting as they do driving balls, and that's a mistake. For most intermediates, the best way to improve your score is by spending more time on the practice green.

One way to make the practice time on the green more enjoyable, and therefore more likely to happen, is to make a game out of it. A simple game is to play against another player on the practice green, going from one hole to another to see who can finish with fewer putts. Another way to make your practice time a challenge is to set a goal for a perfect score on a particular drill, and practice until you reach that goal. If you complete the drill early, leave the green – it's an incentive to do well.

Strategy and course management

The most important golf muscle is the one between your ears. It's the muscle that lets you think your way through each hole, stay focused on your game and form a strategy to get the best score.

Strategy is planning how to use your particular golf skills to play a particular course. Smart strategy lowers scores; lack of a strategy will have you playing too many balls from the rough, hitting too many shots with your weakest clubs or putting so much attention on your long ball that the short game suffers.

Using strategy to play a course is called course management. Course management means that you think about what you are about to do *before* you do it. For example, if you are teeing up on a narrow fairway with deep woods on either side, and you are in the habit of slicing or hooking the ball, it is time to ask yourself, "What are the chances that I'm going to land this ball on the fairway with my driver. Off the fairway might mean a lost ball in the woods and a one-stroke plus distance penalty. So do I dare use my driver?"

This is the time to swallow your pride and think smart. Ask yourself if your three wood will give you a better chance of landing in the fairway. A five wood, seven wood, long or even medium iron might be a better choice if your slice has been quite bad on a particular day. On narrow fairways, choose the club that you are confident can get the maximum distance and stay in the fairway. Penalty strokes are a big contributor to high scores.

If you are sustaining penalty strokes when using your driver, take it out of the bag before you go to the course; that way you won't be tempted to use it.

Even if you don't lose a ball and pay the penalty, a long inaccurate shot can also cause problems. A shot may land in the second cut of rough or end up with a tree between the ball and hole, forcing a pitch-out. The saying "long and wrong" applies to many shots made off the tee.

Before walking up to the tee box, you should always check out the layout of the hole either from the score card or the diagram board marking the hole number. You may also buy yardage books at many pro shops that give advice on how to play each hole. If your playing partners are familiar with the course and you are not, don't hesitate to ask for advice. If the course is unfamiliar to you, make use of any help available.

STRATEGY

Strategy doesn't have to be complicated. Here are a few examples of good strategy:

- Today I'm going to avoid penalty shots. Whenever the chance to incur a penalty arises, I'm going to play conservatively.
- In the past I've three-putted too many greens. Today, I'm going to focus on lining up my putts more carefully.
- I haven't been chipping the ball close enough to the hole to give myself the chance of a one-putt very often. Today, I'm going to take more time to figure out how I want my chips to play.
- I have had a disastrous score on the fifth hole. Now I'm going to club way back and just flop the ball up the fairway even if it means a bogey.
- The wind is blowing hard today, so I'm going to make a conscious effort to keep the ball low.

One of the saddest tales of poor course management occurred in 1996 when Greg Norman gave up a six-stroke lead on the last nine holes of the Masters to lose to Nick Faldo by five strokes. Rather than change his strategy from an aggressive style to a conservative one and preserve a solid lead, Norman attempted to increase his lead and in the process made some fatal mistakes.

The moral of this story, of course, is that smart golfers are prepared to change strategy depending on course conditions and the nature of their play on a particular day.

KNOW THE COURSE

The first part of course management is to know as much as possible about the course you are about to play, especially if it is the first time you are playing it. Ask questions when you pay for your golf game: What are the general conditions on the course? How busy is it? From the answers, you will be able to determine that the course is wet or dry or whether a tournament has given the green a beating.

Look at the score card and see how much information is shown about each hole. Ask if yardage books are available – they are worth paying a couple of dollars for the information. Ask how the yardage is indicated on the course. Part of the starter's job is to inform golfers of the condition of the course and any local rules. You may find out that winter rules are in effect and that "pick, clean and place" is allowed. Many courses have free drops for errant balls on certain holes.

Rangers can be a font of information on any particular hole. Part of a ranger's deal includes their playing the course for free; so they always know the course. Don't be afraid to ask "What's the best way to play this hole?" When they tell you, give it a try. You may have just saved yourself a stroke.

If you play overseas, you might well be required to have a caddie accompany you on the course. Again, get advice from the people who know the course.

Ask how long the course plays – sometimes it's not to the advantage of high handicappers to play from the white tees. On long holes, you are going to be hitting driver/fairway wood anyway, which wood doesn't matter. Many long-ball hitters like to play from the white tees because they can get within short iron range of the green from them. But sometimes it might be to your advantage to play the blue tees. Just don't start trying to kill the ball because you're further back; play your regular game.

KNOW YOURSELF

While this existential concept is probably true for all of life, it is especially valuable on the golf course. Smart players know the strengths and weakness of their own game, and use them to advantage. Ask yourself:

- How much distance do I get with each club? (You should have a general knowledge of this from the driving range, but be prepared to modify this to handle particular days and the effect of wind and slope.)
- Which clubs are most reliable – for me? (It's the rare player who can hit the woods and irons with equal reliability. When it counts, choose a club that you can depend upon.)
- How can I get my concentration back? (You have your own tricks – use them.)
- How can I use my slice or draw on this hole?
- How can I use the sand trap to my advantage, or do I need to stay well away?
- How can I get to the best part of my game? (A long-ball hitter may get to the green in one, but if you don't drive that well, go easy on the drive and plan your fairway shot to get you as close to the flag as possible. A good putt, and the hole will likely be yours.)

Strategic golfing doesn't involve skills you're still developing; it makes use of the skills you already have at your disposal. Think before you hit.

RHYTHM OF PLAY

As you play through the fairway, always be ready to play when it is your turn. Even if the course doesn't expect "ready golf," don't waste everyone's time by thinking when it's time to swing. Analyze your options *before* you reach your ball. Get your club selection out of the bag *before* it is your turn to play. Wait at your own ball rather than wandering around the fairway socializing with your partners. This will ensure that you don't have to rush over to your ball to make a quick club selection at the last minute. You also will not hold up your partners and the groups behind you.

The net result of staying focused on the next shot is that you control the pace of your game and have a better chance of hitting a good shot. Hopefully your partners and the players in front and behind will be on the same wavelength. There's nothing more distracting than feeling rushed during a game, and nothing to break concentration more than too much time waiting to play a hole.

Greens When you are hitting an approach to a green, have an idea of how much green you have to work with. This can help you decide whether or not to pitch or chip. Also, before you hit towards the green, confirm the flag stick placement. Then you'll know to adjust the yardage to compensate for a flag stick at the front or back of the green. Similarly, when hitting out of a sand trap, think about how much green you have to play with. You may decide to hit the ball away from the hole so that you stay on the green, not fly by the hole and off the other side of the green. These decisions can save you strokes.

Keeping track of your game It is useful to have a record of your progress. Although score cards are the most obvious way of keeping track, you can also keep a journal or notebook. On a score card, it is a good idea to mark down the number of putts on each hole and also the number of penalty strokes and the holes where they were incurred. This information can be transferred to a notebook and you can add in your reflections on your strengths and weaknesses for that particular day. You may even want to add notes on practice sessions.

PLAY BY THE RULES

The rules of golf were created to help players keep moving forward during a round of golf when they encounter difficult situations. Many of the rules involve penalties, but they also present opportunities for a smart golfer. Knowing the rules will give you options that may keep your score intact. Here are a few examples of rules that can help when you get into trouble.

UNPLAYABLE LIE, Rule 28

Sometimes your ball will land in a spot from which it is nearly impossible to play. You may attempt to hit the ball out, which usually results in several swats that go nowhere – and when you finally get the ball out you've added two or three strokes to your score. The options under Rule 28 state that a player may declare a ball unplayable at any place on the course except in a water hazard. At that point, the ball may be: (1) dropped and played as near as possible to the original position that it was played from, (2) dropped two club's length from where it lies but not closer to the hole, or (3) dropped behind the spot where it lies, on a line with the hole, as far back as the player wishes. The penalty for this is one stroke. One stroke is better than two or three.

IMBEDDED BALL, Rule 25.2

If a ball is embedded in its own pitch mark, it may be lifted and cleaned. Then it may be dropped as close to the pitch mark as possible but no nearer the hole. This a free drop, no penalty.

INTERFERENCE, Rule 25.1

If your ball lands in casual water (temporary ponding on the fairway, ground under repair or a hole made by an animal), you may take relief by lifting and dropping the ball as close to the interference as possible but not closer to the hole. Free drop, no penalty. You may take relief in this situation even if your ball is not in the interference, but your *feet* would be if you set up to hit the ball.

MOVEABLE OBSTRUCTIONS, Rule 24.1

If your ball lands on or near a moveable obstruction such as a rake, the obstruction may be moved. If the ball moves during the moving of the obstruction, your ball may be replaced without penalty. If the ball is in or on the obstruction, it may be lifted and dropped no closer to the hole with no penalty.

IMMOVEABLE OBSTRUCTIONS, Rule 24.2

If a ball lies in or near an immoveable obstruction and the obstruction interferes with your swing or stance, the ball may be lifted and dropped without penalty.

There are many other rules that can help you get around the course. Make it your business to become knowledgeable about them.

Course management is figuring out how to play a course with your ability and the information at hand. This is a part of the game that many high handicappers neglect and yet it is a way to lower scores with very little work. Start thinking and start scoring.

CHAPTER EIGHT

Equipment

Equipment can make a great deal of difference in a golfer's score - this includes not only clubs but items such as balls, shoes and gloves. The entire market for golf and golf products has been expanding rapidly, so it pays to keep up-to-date on new innovations that can lower your handicap. On the other hand, it is wise to be dubious about many new golf products heavily publicized on television. Some of them are just gimmicks that will empty your wallet and wreak havoc on your game.

Nonetheless, there has been a steady improvement in golf equipment over the years. In this chapter, we'll review some of what's available with an eye on what can lower your score.

THE RIGHT SET OF CLUBS

According to the rules of golf, you are allowed to have 14 clubs in your bag. The choice is important - in order to shoot a lower score you need clubs that will produce the highest percentage of good shots. Because there are more clubs available than the standard 14, you should pick and choose a selection to fit the kind of shots that produce the best results. Once you arrive at a set that suits you, take extra clubs out of the bag so that you won't be tempted to use a club that will not produce a high-success shot.

Getting your clubs fitted can help lower your score. Besides the fine tuning that regular fitting provides, there may be other reasons to get custom-fitted. If you have an unusual physical characteristic, such as short or long arms, or large or small hands, you may benefit from a fitting. If all else fails to correct chronic hooking or slicing, a fitting might help. Pro shops and golf stores have machines to measure you, your swing and your clubs. They also have equipment to alter your clubs if your game changes over time.

Many golfers regularly replace their clubs to take advantage of the latest technology, or in the hope that new clubs will automatically improve their game. While the second is not always true (and it takes two to six months, at least, to get used to a new set of clubs), there's no question that technology has made today's golf equipment better than ever.

Shafts Shafts are usually made of steel, aluminum or graphite and vary in both length and flex. Today's graphite shafts are lighter than others and have a greater "whip" action than metal shafts. They therefore produce greater club-head speed and more distance, but they also magnify the effect of mishits. Steel shafts are consistently more accurate than graphite. If accuracy is a problem for you, stick with steel shafts.

Shaft flexes:

L–flex	very flexible	most women
A–flex	flexible	senior golfers and strong women
R–flex	medium flexible	average hitters
S–flex	stiff	strong hitters
X–flex	extra stiff	exceptionally strong hitters

Regular flex is fine for most golfers; however, if you feel that flex is a factor in poor distance or accuracy, you may wish to try other shafts at your pro shop. Faster swings will benefit from a stiffer flex and slower swings will benefit from a more flexible shaft. Having your swing analyzed by a pro is probably the best way to get the shaft that is best for your current swing and level of play.

Shaft length varies with each club. The shaft for a driver may be 43 inches and the shaft for a wedge may be 35½ inches, though shaft lengths are usually about two inches shorter for women. For more information on shaft lengths for specific clubs, refer to the section that follows on clubs. A change in shaft length will alter the swing weight of a club. As well, the flex of a shaft may be changed if it is shortened at the tip. Getting the proper shaft length is a part of having your clubs fitted – not a procedure that can be done at your local hardware or department store.

Since the cost of a new set of clubs may vary from a few hundred to several thousand dollars, it pays to get a set fitted for you that will last for a number of years.

Grips Leather was used in early club construction and is still a favorite material with many golfers. Rubber grips came into use just before World War II. A variation of the plain rubber grip is the stripped rubber grip that looks like a tire that has had its rubber worn off and is showing the cords. This gives a good grip even when wet. Shortly after World War II, composite grips became popular. They were lighter than pure rubber grips and were easier on the hands. Most grips today are a form of composite grip. The shape and taper of grips is pretty much the same for all products.

The only way to select a grip is to try the various styles at your local golf store. The most obvious criteria for an acceptable grip is whether or not it feels comfortable to you. A larger grip may hinder wrist action and therefore release of the hands on the downswing.

You should re-grip your clubs when the current grips become hard, shiny or difficult to hold. Remember that part of a good swing is a light but firm grip on your club; this can't be done if your grips have to be squeezed like a baseball bat.

CLUB HEADS

Club heads for woods were once made of real wood, hence the name. Today, however, except for a small number of club heads made from persimmon or laminated maple, most heads for woods are made of metal. Common metal alloys for woods include aluminum, stainless steel and titanium. There are also composite heads made of graphite or Kevlar. The current rage for titanium drivers is due to the fact that a pure titanium head adds 20 yards, or so, to the drives of most golfers. Whether the extra yardage for a stroke that may constitute 15 percent of your game is worth the extra cost is up to you and depends on your budget.

Iron heads are manufactured by forging or casting the metal. Forging, used for less expensive clubs, involves dropping a metal dye on a sheet of steel with enormous force. The dye is in the general shape of the club head and the club is then finished by grinding, sanding, chrome plating and sand blasting.

Casting is a more expensive but better process for producing a club head. The technology of casting provides for greater detail and more precision in the creation of grooves. Most importantly, casting allows the manufacturer to change the weight distribution on the club head. This has been a great benefit to all levels of golfers, but especially to high handicappers. The casting method of manufacture has introduced the terms "cavity back," "peripheral weighting" and "heel-and-toe weighting." Cast heads are made from stainless steel; therefore no chrome plating is required and the heads won't chip or rust. The "lost wax" or "investment" casting process is a long and labor-intensive one, but the final product is a worthwhile investment for any golfer. Cavity back, peripheral-weighted club heads will be more forgiving than forged club heads. Shots hit off the center of the club face will not fly off-line as far as with forged heads.

For irons, the markings on the club face are regulated by the USGA. The result of these regulations is that most irons have square or V-shaped grooves of a certain size and configuration. Grooves are important because they impart spin to the ball. Spin affects the flight and the roll of a ball after landing, depending on how it was hit. You should keep the grooves clean while you're playing, either with the small tools available for this or by scraping with a tee.

Parts of a club head

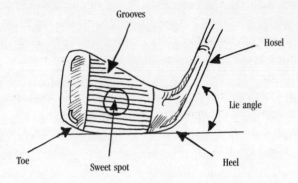

Grooves

Hosel

Lie angle

Toe

Sweet spot

Heel

Lie angle The angle on the sole from the front to back on a club. It is important to have your clubs checked and adjusted if necessary for correct lie angle because incorrect lie angle can dramatically affect your shots. A correct lie angle is most important on short irons because an incorrect lie angle is magnified by the greater loft of the face. If you are having some inexplicable problems with your irons – from five to wedges – you may benefit from having the lie angle of your clubs checked. It's quick and usually free.

How incorrect lie angle can cause problems
(Angles are exaggerated in the illustrations.)

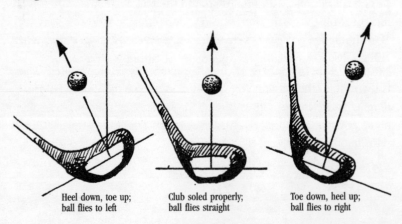

Heel down, toe up;
ball flies to left

Club soled properly;
ball flies straight

Toe down, heel up;
ball flies to right

Sweet spot The spot on the face of the club that, when it strikes the ball, achieves the best result. You can check the sweet spot on any club by holding it between your thumb and forefinger with the face of the club towards you. Begin tapping the face with your other forefinger, starting at the outside of the club and working your way towards the center of the club face. As you tap, you will notice the club swinging away and twisting the shaft with each tap; however, as you approach the center of the club, the swings and twists will decrease until there is no twist and the club swings only straight back. The taps will feel solid. At this point, you've hit the sweet spot.

Some golfers feel as if they have had a religious experience when they swing a club on plane, hit the ball on the sweet spot and the ball flies further than usual with the correct fade or draw. Unfortunately, striking the ball off-center, away from the sweet spot, causes the club to twist and reduces both accuracy and distance. Modern clubs are built to forgive mishits, but it's still best to hit the ball on the sweet spot.

 You can check where you are striking the club face by applying powder, tape or patches especially made for that purpose. If you're not hitting the sweet spot, it's time to go back to work on your swing.

Bounce A design of the sole of the club where the trailing edge is lower than the leading edge. Bounce prevents the club head from digging into sand or allows a club to cut through deep grass. The greatest bounce is found on sand wedges and lob wedges. Clubs with less bounce are used on normal turf or from coarse sand.

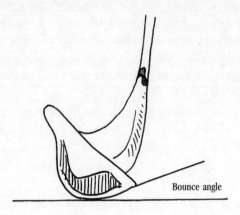

Bounce angle

Swing weight The relationship of the weight of the club head to the weight of the grip end of the club. A special machine that looks like a balance-beam scale measures swing weight. Swing weights are indicated by a letter/number system: theoretically the letters range from A to G, but for practical purposes the swing weight of golf clubs fall in the C to D range (other weights being too light or too heavy for golf clubs). The weight description is further refined by breaking down the letters C and D into 10 finer grades, 0 to 9. Women's clubs are graded form C-2 to C-8 and men's clubs are rated from D-4 to D-8. Swing weights vary by about two grams at a time. If you want to feel how a particular club would feel with more swing weight, you can tape small pieces of lead tape about the weight of a dime (about three grams) to the head.

Swing weight is influenced by factors such as club-head weight, the length of the shaft, shaft and grip weight, and the overall weight of the club. Changing swing weights is an expensive procedure, so it is better to try out and buy a set of clubs with a swing weight that suits you.

Face angle Refers to the angle of the face of the wood's club head in relation to the target when the club is properly grounded. It is possible to manufacture a club with an open or closed face – angled slightly in or out from a perfect perpendicular to the target line. Golfers who slice or hook the ball might get some relief from buying woods that have open or closed faces. But it is a much better idea to reduce slicing and hooking by correcting your swing so you can use clubs with a square face.

WOODS
Approximate shot distances for woods
These are average on-the-fly distances. You might get from 10 to 20 more yards' bounce and roll, depending on how the shot is hit.

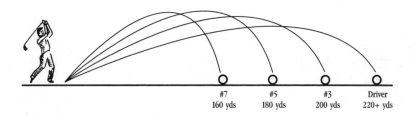

	#7	#5	#3	Driver
	160 yds	180 yds	200 yds	220+ yds

Standard shaft length and loft for woods
Note that the loft of particular clubs will vary from one manufacturer to another.

	For men	*Loft*	*For women*	*Loft*
Driver	43 in.	11°	41 in.	13°
Two wood	42½ in.	14°	40½ in.	15°
Three wood	42 in.	17°	40 in.	17°
Four wood	41½ in.	20°	39½ in.	21°
Five wood	41 in.	22°	39 in.	23°
Seven wood	40 in.	26°	38 in.	27°

Driver Most players use a driver (one wood) to hit the ball off a tee on par fours and fives and, occasionally, on a long par three. It is, therefore, one of the clubs most players will be using about 16 times per game.

However, unless you are consistently hitting the ball over 200 yards and staying in the fairway, you may want to consider leaving the driver out of the bag until you have mastered it. Another club, such as a three wood, will give you more accuracy and sometimes as much or more distance as the driver. Many women, for instance, will get better results by mastering the three-wood than by struggling with a driver for the extra 20 yards it might give them if properly hit.

If you are looking for a new driver, be sure to try out many versions before you settle on one. Most pro shops will have a selection of clubs that may be taken to a range and tried out. Alternately, golf equipment shops may have a net set up into which you can drive balls. A longer shaft gives a wider swing arc, provided that the club is being swung at the same speed as a club of shorter length. The net result should be more distance. However, if you are having trouble with accuracy, you may want to try a normal or shorter-than-normal shaft. This will allow for a more up-and-down swing and therefore a more straight-through-the-ball impact leading to straighter drives.

Driver technology changes yearly – as if another few yards based on the first shot will make a big difference in your game. It won't. Rather than change drivers as often as cars, you might be better off mastering the equipment you have and working to improve the *skills* for the rest of your game.

 The loft of drivers varies from 7–11° or more. If you are having trouble getting the ball up in the air, use a driver with more loft.

Three wood As mentioned above, many golfers benefit from using the three wood off the tee. It's easier to hit with than a driver and the ball will rise up faster due to the increased loft. On par fives and long par fours, the three wood is often the club of choice for the second shot if you are on the fairway. On good lies *off* the fairway, the three wood is also a reasonable choice. If the lie is not so good, it is better to go to a more lofted club such as a five wood.

Five wood Some golfers carry a three wood and a four wood, the four wood being used off the fairway in the deep rough or when less distance and more height is required than the three wood would give. Since you are limited by the number of clubs you can carry in the bag and the distance between a three wood and a four wood is not that great, it is usually more useful to have a five wood in your bag. The five wood will be even better in deep rough and will give another option when the three wood is definitely too much club.

A five wood can replace a two iron and a three iron. Most middle-level golfers will find that these woods are much easier to hit than long irons.

Seven wood Sometimes called "the wimp club" by golfers who can crush long irons without a second thought, the seven wood can still be a deadly weapon in your arsenal. Imagine you're about 160 yards out in the deep rough. On the fairway, you might use a four or five iron, but in the rough these clubs aren't going to get the job done. In this situation the seven wood can come to your rescue. The high loft and wood-shaped head will cut through grass and launch your ball high into the air – a shot that has a good chance of holding the green.

Woods beyond the seven For the reasons discussed above, higher-loft woods have become very popular. Many golfers are carrying nine, eleven and thirteen woods. Remember, the officials don't ask you how you got that low score, just what score you achieved. If high-loft woods work for your swing, use them.

IRONS

Approximate shot distance for irons

These are average on-the-fly distances. You might get from 10 to 20 more yards' bounce and roll, depending on how the shot is hit.

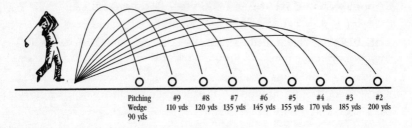

Pitching Wedge 90 yds	#9 110 yds	#8 120 yds	#7 135 yds	#6 145 yds	#5 155 yds	#4 170 yds	#3 185 yds	#2 200 yds

Standard shaft length and loft for irons

Note that the loft of particular clubs will vary from one manufacturer to another.

	For men	*Loft*	*For women*	*Loft*
One iron	39½ in.	17°	37½ in.	18°
Two iron	39 in.	20°	37 in.	20°
Three iron	38½ in.	23°	36½ in.	21°
Four iron	38 in.	25°	36 in.	25°
Five iron	37½ in.	28°	35½ in.	29°
Six iron	37 in.	32°	35 in.	33°
Seven iron	36½ in.	46°	34½ in.	37°
Eight iron	36 in.	40°	34 in.	41°
Nine iron	35½ in.	43°	33½ in.	45°
PW	35½ in.	48°	33½ in.	50°
SW	35½ in.	55°	33½ in.	56°
LW	35½ in.	60°+	33½ in.	60°

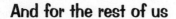

And for the rest of us

One of the reasons pro golfers like Tiger Woods, Vijay Singh and John Daley shoot such low scores is that they can smash a 300-plus yard drive and then use a wedge or short iron onto the green. We lesser mortals don't drive the ball 300 yards. Most golfers are happy if they can drive the ball 200-plus yards and land in the fairway. That's really all you need to play excellent amateur golf.

Long irons The one, two and three irons are hard to hit. As Lee Trevino said as he walked down a fairway holding his one iron in the air during an impending lightning storm, "Even God can't hit a one iron." What's more, because the trajectory of a ball hit with a long iron is relatively low, long iron shots are hard to hold on the green. Medium to high handicappers will get better results by leaving the long irons out of their bags and buying extra woods as discussed above. A golfer is always better off playing with clubs that work reliably.

Four, five and six irons All golfers should carry five and six irons; a four iron may not be necessary if you have a seven wood in your bag. The five and six irons will be used quite often for an approach shot to the green from about 140 to 160 yards. This should be one of your basic shots. Practice it well and you will hit many greens in regulation. The higher loft of these medium irons gives enough height to hold greens, especially if you hit down on the ball to impart backspin.

Short irons Better than making your approach to the green with a middle iron is to have the great joy of hitting a short iron to the green. The short irons hit your ball higher with more backspin and have a tendency to make a nice ball mark on the green, then bounce and roll a short distance. Golf can be a grand game when hitting with these clubs.

Many golfers develop a love for a particular iron when approaching the green – it becomes their "bread-and-butter club." For many, this becomes a seven iron, which may be hit fully from about 150 to 130 yards out depending on how powerfully you hit the ball. Golfers may also hit the seven iron closer in, providing they use a three-quarter or half swing. Confidence in how well you can hit a certain club goes a long way towards hitting good golf shots. If you have developed this relationship with a particular club, by all means continue. Don't feel that just because you are at a certain yardage you must use a certain club.

WEDGES — PITCHING, SAND AND LOB

The job of the wedges is the same as that for medium and short irons – to get the ball as close as possible to the pin for the chance to one-putt. The wedges are also used to get out of sand traps and deep rough around the green. The most important thing to know about wedges is how far can you hit a particular wedge from a particular type of lie and ground cover. As has been said many times in this book and elsewhere, most of your shots are taken around or on the green. Become a great wedge player and your score will drop accordingly.

PUTTER

The putter is the most important club in your bag – you take the most shots with it, you require the greatest accuracy from it and it will give you the most frustration if you use it poorly. Unfortunately, there is no single putter design that is right for all golfers. The only person who can decide which putter is best is you.

There are three factors to consider when buying a putter – shaft length, shape of the head and weight. The standard length for the shaft on a putter is 35 inches, however some golfers putt very successfully with very short-shafted putters (33 inches or even less). Putter heads are generally of two designs, the blade and the mallet head. This is purely a personal choice. A heavier putter gives more feel than a lighter putter. You'll only know which putter is best by trying them.

Some new putters have been developed with a softer center core. These are uncannily quiet when they tap the ball, and they claim to have various other advantages, but only you can tell whether they will really improve your putting.

A suggested selection of clubs:
driver, three wood, five wood, seven wood, three iron, five iron, six iron, seven iron, eight iron, nine iron, pitching wedge, sand wedge, lob wedge, putter

BALLS

It's okay to use scuffed old balls or found balls when you are playing a practice round or hitting over water with a good chance of drowning a ball, but if you are playing a serious game of golf, you should use new or almost-new balls. New balls have all the compression built in by the manufacturer, and when hit properly they will fly farther than an old ball.

It is especially important to play with the same make and model of ball throughout a game. Consistency is the key to good golf, so why use different balls that might have different characteristics in play? You will also benefit from finding a ball you like and using it all the time. That way, when you get out on the course, you will know what to expect.

Heat is not good for balls – it reduces their compression and therefore their performance. If the trunk of your car gets overheated on hot days, take out the balls and put them in the air-conditioned part of the car.

In order to conform to the USGA specification, balls can be no smaller than 1.68 inches in diameter and no heavier than 1.62 ounces; they can go no faster than 250 feet per second and carry and roll no further than 280 yards when tested on a mechanical device known as "Iron Byron" (named after Byron Nelson). As with most golf equipment, the variety in ball selection is enormous. There are one-, two- and three-piece balls, there are long-distance balls and there are "feel" balls with special coverings like "Balata." Most middle-level golfers will benefit from a ball that gives them maximum distance. Low handicappers benefit from the control they derive from using a Balata-type ball.

SHOES

Get a pair of comfortable, waterproof golf shoes. Why? Because your swing is based on your feet. The rotation that your feet must do is better accommodated by a golf shoe than a running shoe.

Hard spikes are going the way of the dodo because they not only chew up greens, but they aren't good for your feet. Soft spikes are great for greens and for feet. If you haven't switched over from hard to soft spikes, you're in for a treat. Also, if you have any kind of foot problem, get running-shoe-style golf shoes that have air cushioning. If your feet feel better you'll play a better game of golf.

GLOVES

A golf glove protects your hand and fingers, especially if you hit a fat shot that jars the hands. A glove also provides extra gripping power for your left hand. When buying a golf glove, fit is very important. A new golf glove should be quite tight; it will stretch a little during use. Any bagginess in a golf glove will have a negative effect on your grip.

CHAPTER NINE

Lessons and practice

There are many different ways to learn golf. Some golfers learn from a relative or friend, others are self-taught, still others begin with professional lessons. Provided that the relative or friend has the necessary patience and skill, this kind of lesson can work well for beginners. As many parents know, a golf course is a great place to spend time with your kids.

Many golfers are self-taught. After some early direction, they manage to get further information from golf books and magazines, and by watching golf on television. A person can get quite good following this approach, and many golfers who have brought themselves along to the point of being a good intermediate player are loathe to let anyone mess with their game.

But sooner or later, everyone needs the assistance of a golf pro in developing their game. While many skilled golfers will offer to help those who are less developed, they often don't understand either teaching or the way golf skills develop over time. While a self-taught golfer can pick up many ideas and tricks, it's virtually impossible for him to assess his own swing and other skills. A golf professional, certified by the Canadian Golf Association, knows how to play golf and knows how to teach – the essential combination to help you.

THE LOCAL PRO

A good golf pro will take into account your age, physical condition, level of experience and your personal goals before suggesting changes or drills. This is impossible to accomplish in a single lesson, so most pros will insist on a minimum package of three, five or 10 lessons so that what's taught is relevant to your game.

Why don't more people take golf lessons? It could be that the word "lesson" is equated with unhappy school memories, but it's better to think of golf lessons as getting coached by an expert on ways to improve. Usually the material covered will be determined by you, after discussion with the pro, and can focus on those aspects of your game that most need work. Also, golf lessons are usually fun. Think of the time spent taking golf lessons as personal quality time – an investment that will cut strokes off your future golf games.

 A lesson is not a practice session; a lesson gives you something to practice.

It is important to understand the teaching process before you begin a set of lessons. Good teachers often use the three C's – Check, Coach and enCourage. This means they will observe your technique, demonstrate the correct technique and give you positive support for your efforts. Since all teachers are not created equal, it is up to you to assess the pro early in the process to determine if you have a good match. If you feel uncomfortable, change pros.

A three-lesson package can cover only a part of your game. If possible, a weekly lesson over the season will allow the pro to work on every aspect of what you do. This is the best approach if you're in a slump and feel a general overhaul of your technique is called for. One such schedule might go like this:

- three weeks on overall swing
- three weeks on sand shots
- three weeks on putting
- three weeks on hitting off the grass
- three weeks on chipping and pitching

CLINICS AND SCHOOLS

Many golf courses now offer group lessons and clinics to members and others who sign up. In a clinic, the pro will work with a small group of golfers on a particular aspect of the game – putting, pitching, sand play. There will be some general instruction followed by a chance to try out techniques on the driving range or practice area. Sometimes the pro will have sophisticated electronic or video equipment to analyze your swing; sometimes the instruction will feel more like a golf school.

Weekend or weeklong schools provide for intense golf instruction. Ordinarily there is a group lesson in the morning, some practice time and a game of golf each day. Sometimes these are combined with luxurious resort accommodations in Quebec, Ontario or British Columbia. In the winter, weeklong golf getaways offer both lessons and regular golf games in locales that range from Mexico to the Bahamas.

These golf schools often use the name of a famous professional golfer as a lure to bring in paying customers. The famous pro, ordinarily, has had a hand in setting up the lesson structure but is only rarely onsite to give *you* actual instruction. Instead, you'll find the same range of pros that you would at your local golf course, but all of them following a particular methodology (and charging a premium for that).

How effective are these intensive experiences in improving your game? Much depends on your seriousness in approaching the lessons, the instruction and exactly what kind of improvement your game needs. For every player who comes back with a story of knocking five points off his handicap, there's another who'll say that his natural swing was messed up for a whole season.

PRACTICE

If you take lessons – or if you don't – the only way you'll improve your game is if you practice. After a pro has suggested a modification in your play, you'll need hours of practice on the range before the new approach should be taken onto a course.

To make any practice session profitable, it should be planned and organized. Here are 12 key items:

1. Dress as you would when golfing. Always wear your golf shoes and glove (if you use one).

2. Have an idea of what part of your game you want to practice and how much time you want to spend on it. Always focus on something; otherwise you're just hitting balls.

3. Set goals for success when you practice. For example, you might say, "I'm going to hit sand shots until I get five shots cleanly out." Then stick to your goals – and reap the rewards.

4. In addition to the drills your pro will give you, there are drills in this book you may find useful. You can also make up drills and practice games yourself. Golf magazines always include a section on practice drills.

5. Start a session with easy swings using a five or six iron. Don't go to longer clubs until you start hitting the sweet spot regularly with these clubs.

6. In chapter 1, we discussed the pre-shot routine. In order to make it second nature, be sure to go through your complete pre-shot routine for, say, a quarter of your hits.

7. Once you get your game improving, keep on practicing. If you can't get to a range, you might want to set up a practice area in your backyard or – if you have high ceilings – use foam balls on your carpet at home.

8. At the range, practice from the grass whenever possible. Hitting off mats is second best. From the grass, you can not only hit realistic grass shots, but you'll use a real tee rather than a rubber tube.

9. Most golfers go to the range and hit a bucket of balls with their driver. The couple of shots that they hit sweet might make them feel good, but it doesn't do much for their game. If there is no specific part of your swing to work on, try to hit a variety of shots.

10. You can combine chipping, pitching and sand shots by tossing a bucket of balls into a sand trap and hitting them out, then chipping or pitching them back in.

11. Make putting a number one priority for practice. Some courses allow you to chip onto the green, as well.

12. While practice on a range is a good way to improve your shot, playing practice rounds of golf is another. A practice round gives you the chance to swing your club under real conditions, and includes course management as part of the game. This works best with friends to coach or a pro to help you in your play.

There are, of course, only three principles involved in becoming a better golfer - practice, practice and practice.

CHAPTER TEN

The mental game

Learning all the right techniques, taking lessons, practicing and having the right equipment are not sufficient to improve your score on a consistent basis. Too often, the best preparation for a round goes for naught because players get upset when they flub an easy putt or take a penalty stroke early in a round. For the rest of the game, these kind of mistakes nag at the back of the mind, destroying concentration. The result – a high score.

Keeping a cool head on the course is so important to good scores that some pros take medication to stay calm. Amateurs certainly don't have to go to that extreme; you do however, have to understand how your emotions will affect your score.

There are basically three sets of emotions that arise during a round of golf. The first is the warm fuzzy feeling you get from the pure pleasure of getting out to the golf course – an emotion that stays with you until you hit the first complete stinker of a shot. This is when the second emotion kicks in – anger. At the next bad shot, and the prospect of a dismal day on the greens, a third emotion begins – despair. The only thing that will lift a golfer up out of this morbid state is a blistering drive down the center of the fairway or a dazzling shot from the fairway that lands 18 inches from the hole. Needless to say, golf is an emotional roller coaster; the trick is how to minimize the damage that emotions can do to your score.

Disaster holes When golfers are trying to lower their handicap from the mid-twenties to the mid-teens, double bogies are a problem - but triple and quadruples are a bigger one! To shoot in the mid-eighties you need to make many pars and the occasional birdie to offset the bogies and double bogies you are inevitably going to score.

When disaster strikes and a triple or quadruple bogey is scored, it is very important to get back on track and recover on the next hole. Wallowing in self-pity and self-punishment is going to ruin your concentration and bring doubt and tension into your game. If disaster hits, try to play through the hole as calmly as possible. Throwing clubs and cursing the golf gods is just going to bring on more trouble. If you can't help an emotional outburst, try to make it a humorous one. It's much better to laugh at your own ineptitude than to let depression drag a whole round of golf down.

Once a disaster hole is finished, put it behind you. The next hole is a clean slate. It helps to avoid talking about all the bad things that happened; try to focus on any positive aspects of the hole. For example, if you had a great drive, talk about it, not the seven iron you hit into the pond. If there is nothing good to say about any of your shots, reflect on the great weather, the beauty of the golf course or the pleasure of being away from the worries of the world. Think about what you have to do to score well on the next hole - it will help keep the negative thoughts about the previous hole at bay. If you watch PGA golf, notice how Fred Couples deals with adversity on the course - cool, calm and relaxed. Fred is always smiling.

Negative topics Conversation on the golf course that focuses on the negative will eventually have a negative effect on your playing. Topics to avoid include business, personal, financial and health problems. Nobody wants to hear about your pending divorce, bankruptcy or lawsuits, and you really should be concentrating on you golf.

If your partner starts whining about his state of affairs, try to steer the conversation to more positive topics. It won't help anyone's game carrying on about some unhappy part of your life. Golf courses are a chance to get away from all that. Remember golf is a game - you're supposed to be having fun. Be happy, be positive.

Some bounces are going to go your way and some are not. Get used to it.

Stay focused

Sometimes your golf partners will do their darndest to destroy your mental game – all with your best interests at heart, they'll say. Just remember, ignore the small talk and focus on your game. Decline any offers by others in the foursome to give you advice on your game. Concentrate. Think positively: "Where am I? On the golf course. What am I going to do? Play good golf."

Unreasonable expectations Golf scores improve slowly: it takes a great deal of effort to knock five strokes off a handicap. If you have been shooting in the low nineties, it's unlikely you are going to jump to the mid-eighties without lowering your score point by point over a number of months. Unrealistic expectations can lead to depressing disappointments.

When you go out to play golf, set a realistic goal such as "Today I am going to match my score the last time I played," or "I am going to lower my handicap today by a stroke because I have been practicing my putting every day for two weeks," or "I've been taking lessons, practicing and playing regularly, so I expect to play well today."

It is said that the average golf score is 93. This represents pretty good play since the vast majority of golfers have trouble breaking 100. Breaking 100, on a tough course from the blue tees, is quite an accomplishment. The lower your average score becomes, the harder it is to take it to a lower level. Be realistic in your goals and you won't be disappointed by not reaching an unrealistic one. Great attitude equals great score.

Too many golfers gauge their score by what they see the pros doing on television and what they read in golf magazines. This is ridiculous. Amateur golf and PGA tour golf are two different games.

Professional golfers depend on their success to bring home a pay cheque. Most of them have played since early childhood. They practice a lot, sometimes every day. Their clubs are custom-fitted; they get all the balls they can use. They hire the best teachers to hone their swing and figure out why they are missing those short putts. When they play a tournament, they have a caddie who is often a professional golfer too. The caddies carry their bags, tell them what the yardage is, clean their clubs and commiserate about strategy. The courses they play on are manicured. The fairways and greens are cut to PGA specifications. They know what to expect when they get out there. And if they do everything right, they get rich and famous.

That doesn't sound much like your situation, does it? If pros are shooting sub-par rounds under those circumstances and you are shooting under 100 or maybe under 90 in conditions that pros wouldn't dream of playing, that's a considerable achievement. Give yourself credit for modest success – your livelihood doesn't depend on making or breaking par.

 Birdie temptation

Birdies are hard to get and usually not worth the tension involved in striving for them. High handicappers should focus on scoring par. Every once in a while you will get the chance to putt for birdie, but don't plan for it. Striving to score a birdie on every hole will lead to mistakes, either from hitting the ball too hard or from taking chances that lead to penalties or extra strokes. Go for par and let the birdies happen naturally.

If your opponent scores well There is nothing like an opponent playing exceptionally well or getting a couple of lucky breaks to create a sense of anger or despair, especially if you're struggling yourself. What's important is to ignore what other players are doing and stick to any game plan you may have. If you decided to play conservatively and keep the ball in the fairway, don't start ripping drives off into the trees just because your opponent is hitting the ball long and straight. If your opponent is playing poorly, be sympathetic; hopefully the favor will be returned.

Anxiety Anxiety can lead to poor golf shots. Tension caused by anxiety is said to tighten muscles by seven percent, and this leads to a poor swing. In order to play good golf you need to be relaxed and confident. If you feel anxious, take a couple of deep breaths and shake it off. Don't worry about how well you are going to play; you'll know when you tote up the score at the end of the round.

When you're playing, forget about whether or not you're going to do all those things the pro taught you at the range. If you learned the techniques properly, they will happen naturally; if you didn't, you'll have to go back and practice some more. Let your game unfold, don't force it.

When you are playing a regular round of golf, it's the wrong time to make changes or fix your swing. Work on changes at the driving range. Well-intentioned partners or opponents who try to help a golfer during regular play are not helping at all. In fact they may be creating anxiety in a player who needs concentration and confidence.

A good rule to live by on the course is, don't give advice unless you're asked for it and politely decline advice from players who want to take your swing apart in the middle of a round. Your swing may not be the greatest, but it's all you've got. Get a golf pro to sort out your problems. The pros are trained for it, and they get paid to do it right.

Use visualization A mental exercise that works for the pros can also work for you. Before setting up to make a shot, stand behind the ball and visualize the *perfect* shot. Imagine the ball flying from the club face, rising into the air on a perfect line of flight, landing and bouncing at the right spot and coming to rest right where you want it to. If you put a little effort into this mental exercise, you'll be surprised at the result. You are going to hit the ball sweeter than before and have shots that happen the way you imagined.

Avoid panic An interesting phenomenon that strikes golfers occasionally at all levels is panic - followed by a complete loss of all logic. Panic is often caused by playing a good round and then having an unexpectedly bad shot mess it up. Instead of standing back and taking a deep breath and reviewing the options, a golfer may hit ball after ball into the same hazard. This was well illustrated in the movie *Tin Cup*.

So when you shock yourself with a truly terrible shot, don't panic and start hitting balls one after the other. Stand back and take a break; let other players play first.

Panic can also hit on the green. If you miss a putt you expected to make, don't rush to putt out. Many very short putts are missed this way.

The psychology of golf is much more complicated than the limited discussion here. What's important is to be aware of the negative effects that out-of-control emotions can have on your score, and the positive effects that relaxed, controlled emotions can have on letting you play your best game. Stay cool and hit well.

OVER 100 CLASSIC COLES NOTES ARE ALSO AVAILABLE:

SHAKESPEARE

- Antony and Cleopatra
- Antony and Cleopatra Questions & Answers
- As You Like it
- Hamlet
- Hamlet in Everyday English
- Hamlet – Questions & Answers
- Julius Caesar
- Julius Caesar in Everyday English
- Julius Caesar Questions & Answers
- King Henry IV – Part 1
- King Henry V
- King Lear
- King Lear in Everyday English
- King Lear – Questions & Answers
- Macbeth
- Macbeth in Everyday English
- Macbeth – Questions & Answers
- Measure for Measure
- Merchant of Venice
- Merchant of Venice in Everyday English
- Midsummer Night's Dream
- Midsummer Night's Dream in Everyday English
- Midsummer Night's Dream Questions & Answers
- Much Ado About Nothing
- Othello
- Othello – Questions & Answers
- Richard II
- Richard III
- Romeo and Juliet
- Romeo and Juliet in Everyday English
- Romeo and Juliet Questions & Answers
- Taming of the Shrew
- Tempest
- Twelfth Night

SHAKESPEARE TSE*

- Hamlet T.S.E.
- Julius Caesar T.S.E.
- King Henry IV – Part I T.S.E.
- King Lear T.S.E.
- Macbeth T.S.E.
- Merchant of Venice T.S.E.
- Othello T.S.E.
- Romeo and Juliet T.S.E.
- Taming of the Shrew T.S.E.
- Tempest T.S.E.
- Twelfth Night T.S.E.

*Total Study Edition

LITERATURE AND POETRY

- Animal Farm
- Brave New World
- Catch 22
- Catcher in the Rye, Nine Stories
- Chrysalids, Day of the Triffids
- Crucible
- Death of a Salesman
- Diviners
- Duddy Kravitz and Other Works
- Edible Woman
- Emma
- Fahrenheit 451
- Farewell to Arms
- Fifth Business
- Glass Menagerie
- Grapes of Wrath
- Great Expectations
- Great Gatsby
- Gulliver's Travels
- Heart of Darkness
- Huckleberry Finn
- Iliad
- Jane Eyre
- King Oedipus, Oedipus at Colonus
- Lord of the Flies
- Lord of the Rings, Hobbit
- Man for All Seasons
- Mayor of Casterbridge
- 1984
- Odyssey
- Of Mice and Men
- Old Man and the Sea
- One Flew Over the Cuckoos Nest
- Paradise Lost
- Pride and Prejudice
- Machiavelli's The Prince
- Scarlet Letter
- Separate Peace
- Stone Angel and Other Works
- Street Car Named Desire
- Surfacing
- Tale of Two Cities
- Tess of the D'Urbervilles
- To Kill a Mockingbird
- Two Solitudes
- Who Has Seen the Wind
- Wuthering Heights

THE CANTERBURY TALES

- The Canterbury Tales
- Prologue to the Canterbury Tales Total Study Edition
- Prologue to the Canterbury Tales
- French Verbs Simplified

HOW TO GET AN A IN ...

- Calculus
- Permutations, Combinations & Probability
- School Projects & Presentations
- Senior Algebra
- Senior English Essays
- Senior Physics
- Sequences & Series
- Statistics & Data Analysis
- Trigonometry & Circle Geometry

BIOLOGY

- Biology Notes

CHEMISTRY

- Elementary Chemistry Notes Rev.
- How to Solve Chemistry Problems
- Introduction to Chemistry
- Senior Chemistry Notes Rev.

MATHEMATICS

- Elementary Algebra Notes
- Secondary School Mathematics 1
- Secondary School Mathematics 4

PHYSICS

- Elementary Physics Notes
- Senior Physics

REFERENCE

- Dictionary of Literary Terms
- Effective Term Papers and Reports
- English Grammar Simplified
- Handbook of English Grammar & Composition
- How to Write Good Essays & Critical Reviews
- Secrets of Studying English

**For fifty years, Coles Notes have been helping
students get through high school and university.
New Coles Notes will help get you through the rest of life.**

Look for these NEW COLES NOTES!

GETTING ALONG IN ...
- French
- Spanish
- Italian
- German
- Russian

HOW TO ...
- Write Effective Business Letters
- Write a Great Résumé
- Do A Great Job Interview
- Start Your Own Small Business
- Buy and Sell Your Home
- Plan Your Estate

YOUR GUIDE TO ...
- Basic Investing
- Mutual Funds
- Investing in Stocks
- Speed Reading
- Public Speaking
- Wine
- Effective Business Presentations

MOMS AND DADS' GUIDE TO ...
- Basketball for Kids
- Baseball for Kids
- Soccer for Kids
- Hockey for Kids
- Gymnastics for Kids
- Martial Arts for Kids
- Helping Your Child in Math
- Raising A Reader
- Your Child: The First Year
- Your Child: The Terrific Twos
- Your Child: Age Three and Four

HOW TO GET AN A IN ...
- Sequences & Series
- Trigonometry & Circle Geometry
- Senior Algebra with Logs & Exponents
- Permutations, Combinations & Probability
- Statistics & Data Analysis
- Calculus
- Senior Physics
- Senior English Essays
- School Projects & Presentations

**Coles Notes and New Coles Notes are available at the following stores:
Chapters • Coles • Smithbooks • World's Biggest Bookstore**

NOTES & UPDATES